ICFA Continuing Education
Credit Analysis Around the World

Proceedings of the AIMR seminar "Credit Analysis Around the World"

February 10, 1998
Chicago, Illinois

Carl S. Bang, CFA, *Moderator*
George A. Ashur
Laura Feinland Katz
Sean P. Flannery

David Larson
John Paulsen
Ashwin Vasan

To obtain the *AIMR Publications Catalog,* contact:
AIMR, P.O. Box 3668, Charlottesville, Virginia 22903, U.S.A.
Phone 804-980-3668; Fax 804-980-9755; E-mail info@aimr.org
or
visit AIMR's World Wide Web site at **www.aimr.org**
to view the AIMR publications list.

©1998, Association for Investment Management and Research

All rights reserved. No part of this publication may be reproduced, stored in a retrieval system, or transmitted, in any form or by any means, electronic, mechanical, photocopying, recording, or otherwise, without prior written permission of the copyright holder.

ICFA Continuing Education is published monthly seven times a year in May, May, June, June, July, August, and September by the Association for Investment Management and Research, P.O. Box 3668, Charlottesville, Virginia 22903, U.S.A. This publication is designed to provide accurate and authoritative information with regard to the subject matter covered. It is sold with the understanding that the publisher is not engaged in rendering legal, accounting, or other professional services. If legal advice or other expert assistance is required, the services of a competent professional should be sought. Periodicals postage paid at the post office in Richmond, Virginia, and additional mailing offices.

Copies are mailed as a benefit of membership to CFA® charterholders. Subscriptions also are available at US$100 for one year. Address all circulation communications to ICFA Continuing Education, P.O. Box 3668, Charlottesville, Virginia 22903, U.S.A.; Phone 804-980-3668; Fax 804-980-9755. For change of address, send mailing label and new address six weeks in advance.

Postmaster: Send address changes to the Association for Investment Management and Research, P.O. Box 3668, Charlottesville, Virginia 22903.

ISBN 0-935015-20-5
Printed in the United States of America
June 1998

Editorial Staff
Jan R. Squires, CFA
Book Editor

Elizabeth A. Collins
Editor

Jaynee M. Dudley
Production Manager

Christine E. Kemper
Assistant Editor

Christine P. Martin
Production Coordinator

Lois A. Carrier
Diane B. Hamshar
Composition

Contents

Foreword v
    Katrina F. Sherrerd, CFA

Biographies vi

Overview: Credit Analysis Around the World 1
    Jan R. Squires, CFA

Effective Sovereign Credit Analysis 3
    George A. Ashur

EMU and the Bond Markets of Western Europe 10
    Sean P. Flannery

Eastern Europe 18
    Ashwin Vasan

Africa and the Middle East 26
    David Larson

Corporate Credit Analysis: Latin America 38
    Laura Feinland Katz

Asian Lessons and Outlook 47
    John Paulsen

Self-Evaluation Examination
    Questions 61
    Answers 63

Selected Publications 64

ICFA Board of Trustees, 1997–98

Fred H. Speece, Jr., CFA, *Chair*
Minneapolis, Minnesota

Philippe A. Sarasin, CFA, *Vice Chair*
Geneva, Switzerland

Abby Joseph Cohen, CFA, *AIMR Chair*
New York, New York

Frank K. Reilly, CFA, *AIMR Vice Chair*
Notre Dame, Indiana

Thomas A. Bowman, CFA, *AIMR President and CEO*
Charlottesville, Virginia

Dwight D. Churchill, CFA
Merrimack, New Hampshire

Jon T. Ender, CFA
Chicago, Illinois

Martin S. Fridson, CFA
New York, New York

Thomas L. Hansberger, CFA
Ft. Lauderdale, Florida

Glen A. Holden, Jr., CFA
Golden, Colorado

George W. Long, CFA
Hong Kong

Thomas P. Moore, Jr., CFA
Boston, Massachusetts

George W. Noyes, CFA*
Boston, Massachusetts

I. Rossa O'Reilly, CFA
Toronto, Ontario, Canada

Brian F. Wruble, CFA
New York, New York

ex officio

AIMR Education Committee, 1997–98

Fred H. Speece, Jr., CFA, *Chair*
Minneapolis, Minnesota

Frank K. Reilly, CFA, *Vice Chair*
Notre Dame, Indiana

Terry L. Arndt, CFA
Mount Pleasant, Michigan

Keith C. Brown, CFA
Austin, Texas

Abby Joseph Cohen, CFA
New York, New York

Scott L. Lummer, CFA
Chicago, Illinois

Katrina F. Sherrerd, CFA
Charlottesville, Virginia

J. Clay Singleton, CFA
Charlottesville, Virginia

AIMR Senior Education Staff

Thomas A. Bowman, CFA
President and CEO

Katrina F. Sherrerd, CFA
Senior Vice President

J. Clay Singleton, CFA
Senior Vice President

Terence E. Burns, CFA
Vice President

Julia S. Hammond, CFA
Vice President

Robert R. Johnson, CFA
Vice President

Robert M. Luck, Jr., CFA
Vice President

Craig K. Ruff, CFA
Vice President

Donald L. Tuttle, CFA
Vice President

Barbara L. Higgins
Director

Paul W. Turner
Director

Foreword

The benefits of globally diversifying fixed-income portfolios for return enhancement and risk reduction are well known—so well known that managers may be tempted to think that any non-U.S. bond will provide the touted return enhancement and risk reduction. Not so. To achieve portfolio goals, managers must delve into the nitty-gritty basics of choosing among the wide assortment of debt issues available in the global markets. AIMR developed the continuing education seminar on which this proceedings was based to help in a key element of that selection process: credit analysis.

Credit analysis for non-U.S. debt securities is a different kettle of fish from the kind of analysis that suffices for U.S. debt. As fixed-income portfolio managers around the world increase their investment in non-U.S. debt, they face different legal standards and reporting requirements, sometimes a scarcity of information, and political risk concerns that simply do not exist for the debt of the U.S. government, U.S. agencies, or companies domiciled in the United States. A specific issue today is what are the changes we can expect in European and world bond markets from the implementation of the European Monetary Union.

The authors in this proceedings make clear that the necessary credit analysis cannot be left up to the rating agencies. The agencies face many of the same difficulties managers and investors face, so reliance on their conclusions alone is highly risky. In the final analysis, for credit analysis in the non-U.S markets, managers need attitudes, approaches, frameworks, and tools appropriate to the global arena—all of which are the subject of this proceedings.

The book begins with a discussion of the basic structure and techniques for effective credit analysis of sovereign debt issues. With this structure in mind, readers will be well equipped to follow the subsequent authors' comprehensive dissections of the nuances of credit analysis in Western and Eastern Europe, Latin America, Asia, Africa, and the Middle East.

We are particularly grateful to Carl S. Bang, CFA, for his deftness in moderating the seminar and to Jan R. Squires, CFA, for lending his expertise and professionalism to editing the spoken presentations into written form. We also extend our thanks to all the authors for their cheerful assistance in producing this book: George A. Ashur, Wellington Management Company, LLP; Laura Feinland Katz, Standard & Poor's Corporation; Sean P. Flannery, State Street Global Advisors; David Larson, Moody's Investors Service; John Paulsen, J.P. Morgan and Company; and Ashwin Vasan, OppenheimerFunds, Inc.

The need for those venturing into poorly charted investment waters to minimize credit risk cannot be overemphasized.

Katrina F. Sherrerd, CFA
Senior Vice President
Educational Products

Biographies

George A. Ashur is vice president and director of Fixed Income Research at Wellington Management Company, LLP, where he oversees a staff of analysts involved in the quantitative and qualitative review of both domestic and international bond issuers in all market sectors. He also serves as chair of the firm's bond-screening group, which reviews prospective securities for inclusion in the firm's bond universe. Previously, Mr. Ashur was director of corporate bond research at Chase Securities and a high-yield analyst at PaineWebber. He holds an A.B. in biology and history from the College of the Holy Cross as well as an M.A. in economics and Middle East studies and a Ph.D. in political economics from Harvard University.

Carl S. Bang, CFA, is a senior portfolio manager at State Street Global Advisors, where he is responsible for managing Canadian and international fixed-income portfolios and developing quantitative approaches to global asset allocation. Previously, Mr. Bang was manager of fixed-income and derivative strategies at the Canadian National Pension Fund. He is president of the Montreal Society of Financial Analysts. Mr. Bang holds a bachelor's degree from Windsor University and an M.B.A. from the Schulich School of Business at York University.

Laura Feinland Katz is a director in the Corporate Ratings Department of Standard & Poor's Corporation. She heads the group responsible for Latin American corporate debt ratings, which includes a team of analysts that follows issuers from a diversified group of industries. Previously, Ms. Feinland Katz was vice president in the Bankers Trust Latin American Merchant Banking group, where she was part of the team responsible for bringing first-time issuers to the capital markets. She held a variety of positions in Latin American corporate and trade finance at Marine Midland Bank and at Manufacturers Hanover Trust. Ms. Feinland Katz holds a B.S. in economics from the Wharton School of the University of Pennsylvania and an M.B.A. from New York University.

Sean P. Flannery is a managing director at State Street Global Advisors, where he leads the product engineering team. Prior to joining State Street, he was a senior portfolio manager at Scudder Insurance Asset Management, where he created and implemented investment strategies for a variety of insurance entities, and a portfolio manager at PanAgora Asset Management, where he managed and developed domestic and global fixed-income strategies in both the cash and futures markets. He holds a B.A. in economics from George Washington University.

David E. Larson is a vice president and a senior analyst with the sovereign risk unit at Moody's Investors Service, where he covers several supranational financial institutions, including the International Bank for Reconstruction and Development, the African Development Bank, and the International Finance Corporation. Prior to joining Moody's, Mr. Larson was a country risk analyst at the National Bank for Cooperatives and an economist with the Institute of International Finance in Washington, D.C. He holds a master's degree in finance from the University of Wisconsin at Madison.

John Paulsen is a vice president and the senior fixed-income credit analyst covering sovereign issuers at J.P. Morgan and Company. He leads a team that provides and coordinates research on high-grade and select emerging market sovereign bonds to support primary-market issues and secondary-market trading recommendations. Previously, Mr. Paulsen held positions in senior fixed-income and banking credit with Kidder Peabody and Company, Standard & Poor's Corporation, and National Westminster Bank. He holds a B.S. in international finance from Boston University and an M.B.A. from New York University.

Ashwin Vasan is vice president and portfolio manager for OppenheimerFunds, Inc. He manages the Oppenheimer International Bond Fund and comanages the Oppenheimer Multi-Sector Income Trust and Oppenheimer World Bond Fund. Prior to joining Oppenheimer, Mr. Vasan served as the Latin American economist in the International Corporate Finance Department of Citibank in New York City. He also served as an economics instructor at San Diego State University and Southwestern College. Mr. Vasan holds a B.A. in economics from the University of Nebraska and an M.A. in economics from San Diego State University and is a Ph.D. candidate in economics at the New York University Graduate School of Arts and Sciences.

Overview: Credit Analysis Around the World

Jan R. Squires, CFA
Professor of Finance
Southwest Missouri State University

In a world where advancing technology, political forces, and economic reality are combining to smash the boundaries that divide markets, finding opportunities for diversification and enhanced returns becomes ever more difficult. Information quality improves, asset distinctions blur, correlations increase, and mispricing disappears. But the search for attractive investments continues unabated, and that search has led many global investors who had formerly limited themselves to U.S. debt securities to consider investing in non-U.S. bonds. One result is that many, if not most, well-diversified global portfolios now contain bonds originating from various regions around the world; indeed, the portfolio benefits achieved from adding such bonds have been so widely argued as to be nearly taken for granted.

Investors' decisions to invest in non-U.S. bonds, however, involve credit risk that is not only substantial but also different from the risk of investing in U.S. bonds. Credit analysis for bonds issued by U.S. companies and the U.S. government has become almost routine in nature, but credit analysis for non-U.S. bonds is clouded by a seemingly inexhaustible number of concerns that extend beyond the countries' and companies' abilities and willingness to repay—from problematic legal and accounting standards to political and social unrest to historical and cultural biases. Yet, credit analysis for non-U.S bonds—assessing the risks of nonrepayment or nontimely repayment by non-U.S. issuers—has received decidedly less attention than the benefits to be gained from investing in such bonds.

This proceedings is the product of an AIMR seminar designed to remedy that shortcoming—to remind participants of the sources of credit risk in global bond investing and to highlight best current practices in assessing credit risk. The speakers, drawn from internationally prominent investment firms and the leading credit-rating agencies, are among the profession's "best and brightest" in practicing the art of global credit analysis for both sovereign and corporate issuers. They share with the reader their considerable knowledge—beginning with the sovereign credit analysis process and proceeding through specific regions of the world—to provide a veritable world tour of credit risk factors. Thus together, the presentations constitute an impressive framework for credit analysis of global debt securities.

Sovereign Credit Analysis

George Ashur begins the proceedings by providing a basic structure for performing sovereign credit analysis. A recurring theme in his approach is the need to recognize trends—to go beyond mere seeing to understanding and anticipating. Contending that sovereign analysis is the cornerstone of any global credit analysis process, Ashur sets forth the basic elements of sovereign analysis. He carefully distinguishes sovereign analysis from ordinary economic analysis, and he discusses both quantifiable and qualitative sovereign risk factors. Ashur identifies current trends in sovereign creditworthiness and concludes by emphasizing five tools that can be crucial in anticipating changes in sovereign creditworthiness.

Europe—West and East

Western and Eastern Europe provide a study in contrasts for global bond investors; whereas unity and converging spreads seem likely in Western Europe, diversity and a broad spectrum of risks characterize Eastern Europe.

The European Monetary Union (EMU), a milestone in the development and evolution of global bond markets, is well on its way to full implementation, and Sean Flannery discusses both the emerging benefits and remaining risks that EMU holds for global bond investors. The potential economic impact of the EMU bloc on the world economy is huge indeed. The benefits of unification for capital and bond markets—including freer capital movement, disintermediation, and greater market liquidity—are already appearing, and they will only become more important over time. Flannery cautions that numerous major and minor risks remain to be addressed, however, and that their resolution will determine the EMU's ultimate success.

Ashwin Vasan warns that the debt securities of Eastern Europe are among the hardest in the world for which to perform credit analysis. He classifies East European sovereigns into two credit tiers and discusses key political and economic characteristics that distinguish high-quality from low-quality credits; he devotes particular attention to the outlook for Russia, the key issuer in the low-quality tier. Vasan notes that, despite the difficulties of credit analysis in Eastern Europe, the potential diversification benefits—whether from investment-grade sovereigns, low-quality sovereign issues, or local-currency debt—make the effort worthwhile for a broad spectrum of investors. He closes with an assessment of the likelihood of an East European credit crisis and a brief look at the likely evolution of local-currency debt in the region.

Africa and Middle East

Because the combined Africa/Middle East region contains some 80 countries that differ so greatly, David Larson cautions that generalizations about those countries or their markets are difficult at best. He characterizes the region as being largely resource based, reliant on exports to the developed world, and poorly integrated with the global economy. Participation in bond markets is scant: The rating list of Moody's Investors Service includes only 14 countries in the region. But Larson contends that market forces are at work throughout Africa and the Middle East that will create several opportunities for global bond investors. He discusses in detail the political, economic, demographic, and cultural aspects that make up the credit outlook for South Africa, Turkey, Israel, and the six Arab Gulf countries that are members of the Gulf Cooperation Council.

Latin America

In her discussion of credit risk in Latin America, Laura Feinland Katz focuses on the region's corporate issuers. She advocates a framework for assessing the risks faced by Latin American companies that first considers the sovereign risk—in the form of potential sovereign intervention, country risk, or sovereign policies. To the framework is then added analysis of the company's competitive and financial positions, and Feinland Katz cites numerous corporate examples drawn from throughout the region. She emphasizes that a company's competitive position is a function of its operating efficiency (in light of exchange rates), the regulatory risk, labor environment, country infrastructure, trade barriers, the structure of the local industry, and the company's strategy and ownership. Financial position depends on factors ranging from how the company manages risk and its capital structure to the extent and sources of its financial flexibility.

Asia

The recent Asian financial crisis has many investors questioning their assumptions about sovereign and corporate credit analysis, so John Paulsen's examination of the region is particularly timely. Paulsen contends that the roots of the crisis lie in six key economic factors generally common to the countries of the region. Investors who understand those factors can learn several lessons from the crisis, including the importance to financial markets of a country's internal leverage, credibility of government policies, and banking system risk. Paulsen believes that the long-term outlook for Asia is still positive, although not all countries in the region will recover and develop at the same pace. He concludes his presentation with his detailed views on China, Hong Kong, Indonesia, South Korea, Malaysia, and Thailand.

Effective Sovereign Credit Analysis

George A. Ashur
Vice President and Director of Fixed Income Research
Wellington Management Company, LLP

> Global credit shocks of the past two decades have reaffirmed the importance of sovereign credit analysis. Because of the number and sometimes unfamiliar nature of sovereign issuers, the sovereign analyst faces numerous tasks—from understanding trends in sovereign creditworthiness to identifying key sovereign risk factors and anticipating changes in sovereign credit status.

The reality of sovereign credit analysis is that today's grim headlines about spreads and credit problems around the world are not new news. The past two decades have seen no fewer than four major external shocks to the global markets. In 1982, Mexico and other Latin American countries rescheduled, defaulted, and otherwise roiled the credit markets, which produced the debt phenomenon that ultimately became known as Brady bonds. Rescheduling those Latin American debt loads took nearly 10 years in many cases, and the institutional market ultimately absorbed the repackaged product. In 1990 and 1992, the United States had its own savings and loan crisis, a cathartic event of equal magnitude to the current Asian experience and one that occurred in a market much larger than the Asian markets. The years 1994 and 1995 brought the so-called Tequila Crisis, precipitated by the near default by Mexico on its short-term debt. Finally, 1997 and 1998 will be known as the years of the Asian flu.

An interesting aspect of the human condition is that our life experiences are crystallized by disasters. Whether the disasters are precipitated by the weather, human folly, or our own greed, crises force people to adapt. In the case of sovereign credit analysis, the crises of the past two decades and the pressing need to look more incisively at international issuers have driven the development of analytical techniques and processes that are far superior to those that were available at the beginning of the period. This presentation addresses key aspects of current sovereign credit analysis—recognizing trends in sovereign creditworthiness, basic elements of the analytical process (including quantifiable and qualitative risk factors), and tools for anticipating sovereign credit changes.

Recognizing Trends

The Asian crisis reaffirms a phenomenon common to crisis events: Many observers know what they are seeing as events unfold, but not many truly understand what they see. Many analysts had mountains of data on the Asian markets, but how many really grasped the existence and importance of key trends in those markets? One of the aims of sovereign credit analysis is to develop the ability to recognize trends, to establish a framework for understanding what trends are important and what the trends are revealing about market directions.

Such a framework must reveal, for instance, the current trends in developed and emerging markets—increased privatization, fiscal conservatism, and development of local markets. Increased privatization in both developed and emerging markets has been leading to larger corporate debt issuance than in the past, and this trend is likely to escalate dramatically in the next 10 years. Governments, certainly North American governments but also governments around the world, are emphasizing fiscal conservatism. Even most of the governments in Asia that had catastrophes in the past six months had previously gotten fiscal "religion," which resulted in reduced budget deficits or actual budget surpluses. As the International Monetary Fund (IMF) pressures many of the Asian governments further, the result will be even smaller government deficits, or surpluses, and a reduction in incremental debt issuance. Reduction in debt issuance is certainly expected of the U.S. Treasury, which will be a much smaller debt issuer in the next decade than it was in the past two or three decades. Declining government issuance inevitably leads to the increasing development of local debt markets. This development is already occurring in Argentina and Mexico, where the local markets have resurrected themselves quite nicely. The result will be that local-currency issues will become alternatives to Yankee bonds and Eurobonds.

IMF pressure on a government could have other consequences. It could precipitate social complications that might affect the credit of the sovereign issuer.

Basic Elements of Analysis

Sovereign credit analysis is the cornerstone of any analytical process for global credit and should be the basis for deciding whether to invest in a particular country. What distinguishes sovereign credit analysis from ordinary economic analysis is that sovereign credit analysis adds to pure economic analysis an examination of the elements that are critical to understanding the outlook for a nation—political characteristics, diplomatic relationships, and military, trade, and cultural issues. Certain questions are important to sovereign analysts that might not be so to economists: What is the historical background of the country? Has it been colonized? Has it a tradition of jurisprudence that is similar to Western traditions and that can be translated into a positive attitude about debt and debt repayment? Do religious overtones affect economics? (For instance, Islamic countries do not like debt but will accept leases.)

Conceptually, the two key concerns in sovereign credit analysis are simple: the country's ability to pay off debt and its willingness to pay off debt. *Ability* to pay is relatively easy to determine; *willingness* to pay is much harder to ferret out. A sovereign entity, a prime minister, a finance minister, a central bank governor—any or all can give analysts information concerning the ability to pay. The question is, does the country want to pay? Internal issues, for example, may make a note payment to "foreigners" politically difficult. This "soft" side of debt analysis, had it been executed more seriously or more appropriately, might have led to different investment decisions in Asia, in Latin America, or in certain emerging economies of central Europe.

Sovereign credit analysis consists of assessing four major elements:
- *Liquidity.* Examining the level of foreign reserves and the health of the banking system is particularly critical for emerging market countries. It was probably not performed with sufficient rigor in advance of the South Korean crisis.
- *Characteristics of the external debt.* The mix of debt and the breakdown of external debt, particularly in the context of currency translation, are important factors in a country's ability to pay. What is the country's ability to translate its own currency into U.S. dollars or German marks or Japanese yen to pay off the debt?
- *Internal (fiscal) management.* This element involves analyzing the details of a country's internal management, its fiscal management. What do the fiscal accounts look like, and how can they be translated into an ability to pay?
- *External-accounts management.* The final consideration is the picture for the external accounts. For example, to what degree is the current account running a deficit? What are the components of that deficit, and what makes up merchandise trade? An analyst can accept a deficit in a developing country if it results from capital goods imports but should be concerned if it results from consumer goods imports. In other words, looking at a single ratio or statistic as indicative of a problem may be misleading; interpretation of several pieces of information is necessary to reach a conclusion.

Within any overall framework for sovereign credit analysis are numerous risk factors, either explicit or implicit. The relevant risks can be classified as quantifiable or qualitative.

Quantifiable Risks. Quantifiable-risk assessment involves identifying quantifiable risk factors, evaluating risk implications and the appropriateness of government actions, and developing sound assessment principles.

Risk factors. Identification of quantifiable risk must first address domestic fiscal management at the sovereign level. Analysts should focus on relatively simple measures, such as deficit to GDP and the magnitude of unfunded pension liabilities.

Issues of domestic policy, the costs of these domestic policies, and the efficacy of domestic fiscal management cannot be assessed in a vacuum. For example, in analyzing Brazil's sovereign credits, one must take into account that Brazil has an enormous deficit problem with its social security system. What would change that social security system to the point where the deficit would not be a problem? The answer is: only a compromise between 7 or 8 of the 35 political parties in Brazil. And such a development is probably not realistic in the next year.

A second aspect of quantifiable-risk assessment is researching a country's external accounts and need for nondomestic currency, a task that can be difficult indeed. As the Asian crisis unfolded, many analysts saw the need for such information, but the availability of detailed information and the quality of information was a real and binding constraint. Nonetheless, recent events have affirmed the need for analysts to do the best they can with the information available to develop *pro forma* assessments.

Identifying quantifiable risk also includes breaking down long- and short-term debt by obligor and by maturity. Who in the government owes what to whom and on what schedule? The Mexican Tesobono crisis in 1994 and 1995 and the Korean debt crisis of 1997 and 1998 are prime examples of the importance of this knowledge. In the Tesobono case, a reasonable breakdown of the debt was available, but Tesobono investors apparently did not use it properly. In Korea's case, the government admitted that its published data were not accurate. To learn from both cases, analysts should ask themselves some tough questions: Who was telling the truth? Did we ask the right questions? If we did not ask the right questions, who were the greater fools—the Korean government or us? Did we settle for insufficient answers?

■ *Risk implications of government actions.* The Asian debt crisis is particularly useful in highlighting the importance of evaluating the implications of government actions with respect to quantifiable risks. First, the crisis shows how large-scale debt rescheduling creates a contagion risk to creditors with large regional exposures. Second, the situation cries out for a realistic assessment of the possibilities of recession. Although recession is a distinct possibility in many of these Asian countries, no one seems to have focused on the implications of such a recession for long-term growth. Growth rates that have been 6–8 percent annually since 1993 could, according to some economists, drop by half or more. But analysts' consensus estimates for Malaysia, Korea, and even Thailand, which is clearly in recession now, are still in the 6–8 percent range. Analysts appear to be unwilling to admit the implications of what they are actually seeing. Finally, analysts need to assess whether the fiscal austerity measures, financial restructurings, and corporate and banking system reforms that will result from the policy changes and IMF mandates will be effective or will result in a situation that is worse than the problems that existed. These are the questions that future governments will have to answer, and analysts and investors should not be bashful about continuing to pose such questions.

In the case of the Asian crisis, the various government responses have taken several forms. Some governments, even those not directly affected by this crisis, have taken preemptive steps to improve their external-account deficits; Brazil used increased interest rates to stabilize itself in the fall of 1997, and Chile recently raised short-term rates 150 basis points to stem the growth of its current-account deficit. Some governments have been taking the additional step of reforming their banking sectors. Finally, some governments, although certainly not all, have undertaken the hardest tasks of all: improving financial controls and providing more-transparent disclosures. This last point is particularly important; it seems to be difficult indeed for some governments to be honest about what they owe and how they intend to repay it. The execution of all the IMF mandates has led to a return of investor confidence, albeit weak in comparison with confidence before the crisis.

■ *Basic principles in assessments.* Any system for quantifiable-risk assessment must rest on sound principles. A basic issue is comparability of data. Making "apples-to-apples" comparisons among regions, among issuers, and across time is difficult; accounting standards differ, and levels of disclosure are not uniform. One problem that can be addressed is analysts' apparent fear of asking for what they really want and need. An important challenge for analysts is to hold issuers to a much higher level of disclosure than in the past. When analysts can acquire up-to-date, verifiable or audited financial statements, they can answer the question of whether they would invest in this entity if it were a domestic issuer.

In addition, analysts have to impress on portfolio managers that these markets have a fluid nature, that events will happen, and that "headline" risk will influence the value of securities; simple credit analysis cannot anticipate all the intricacies of such a dynamic environment.

Finally, rating agencies must be held to a transparent and credible standard. Bashing rating agencies serves no purpose, but the rating agencies need to admit that they, like analysts, do not get the best information, that they are doing the best they can, and that they do, in fact, make mistakes.

The primary necessity for effective analysis is, simply stated, full disclosure. The sound principle of full disclosure will lead to sound results. Full disclosure, in the long run, adds to the liquidity of markets and enlarges issuers' access to the global capital markets. Investors and managers who are investing in countries that are difficult even to locate on the globe will find the investing easier, frankly, if they understand the countries—how their economies work, how they finance themselves, and what their needs are. Full disclosure also allows selectivity among global securities or, in other words, greater diversification of risk. Finally, full disclosure will lead ultimately to the development of new and more-efficient local capital markets. Local capital markets have not developed largely because of lack of demand for them. The local capital markets will develop when global investors have adequate information about the issuers and about the markets themselves.

Qualitative Risks. Qualitative risk assessment takes into account a wide range of risk factors beyond quantitative risks and beyond the factors assessed in traditional economic analysis. Qualitative risk factors range from political and government institutions to natural resources and geography.

■ *Political and government institutions.* No risk factor has a greater impact on sovereign creditworthiness than the stance of the ruling government and the political forces in power. Yet, too many sovereign risk analysts could not answer accurately if asked to describe the form of government in, for example, Indonesia. Indonesia has a unicameral legislature with a president who appoints all the legislators. It is nominally a democracy but is run more like a Japanese kingdom. Thailand, in contrast, is nominally a kingdom but is run much more like a Western democracy. These real differences have substantially different implications for creditworthiness, and analysts who retain their ignorance of such differences do so at considerable peril.

■ *Central bank independence.* A truly independent central bank is an enhancement to creditworthiness. So, analysts must be alert to what a particular central bank does, what its responsibilities are, how important it is to the country's economy, and how susceptible it is to political, military, or other kinds of pressure. Two questions are key to determining central bank independence. First, does the bank have a charter that guarantees its independence? For instance, the central bank in the Philippines was only recently separated from the government; it is no longer supervised by the Ministry of Finance but, rather, now has a separate charter. Second, does the central bank have control over the country's foreign currency reserves. A central bank's having its own reserves separate and apart from a finance ministry's control is a sign of the bank's independence. Separate control of reserves also now characterizes the Philippines' central bank.

■ *Sustainable trade patterns.* Analysts need to consider the trade patterns of the sovereign entity issuing debt and whether those patterns are sustainable: Does this issuing country export anything anybody wants to buy? The current dogma that export growth can continue in the Asian market should be questioned: What are these countries making? Who are they selling to? What are the pricing pressures? Who are they going to be putting out of business? Are the Chinese going to let the Koreans undersell them? How many plush toys does the world really need?

■ *Stable social structure.* Analysts need to look carefully at the country's social structures. Are they stable? Massive unemployment arising from their financial difficulties, for example, will destabilize the social structures to some degree in Korea, Indonesia, Malaysia, and Thailand. Which governments are likely to respond with generous (expensive) social programs to compensate for the changes in employment patterns? Analysts need to factor those possibilities into their risk assessments and forecasts.

■ *Military expenditures.* Military expenditures are an important mandate for many governments and may become important in any country where instability takes hold. History has shown that wherever domestic instability rises, the tides of war often follow. Economic and social problems at home are often dealt with, consciously or fortuitously, by war away from home. Although the stability of some regional trade blocs has obviated the need for large, nonproductive investments in the military in the past, such investments may well look attractive in the face of widespread domestic and regional economic problems.

■ *Literacy and productivity.* Western analysts take high rates of literacy and productivity in a population for granted because these rates are extremely high in the United States and the developed countries. But for many (if not most) of the sovereign issuers where risk assessment is critical, neither literacy nor high productivity can be assumed. The reality is that Western investors need to analyze specifically the literacy and productivity levels of the population in the countries of interest to them.

■ *Natural resources and geography.* In assessing qualitative risks, analysts should remember the basic components of countries' comparative advantages and disadvantages. Nothing is more basic to analyzing an issuing country than the country's natural resource base and unique geography. Whether these natural features are a help (rich ore deposits) or a hindrance (rugged terrain), such features do not change and cannot be ignored or assumed away.

Anticipating Changes

As important as historical sovereign debt analysis and risk assessment are, what analysts need even more are some basic tools that will help them anticipate changes in sovereign credit.

The first tool is disclosure, which comes in many forms—issuer registration statements, central bank financial statements, and finance ministry statements. Finding these statements can require extensive research; they are not all reported the same way and often use accounting standards that need to be explained. Nonetheless, issuers do become more forthcoming in the face of investor and analyst pressure. In 1997, for instance, the Republic of Lebanon came out with two new debt issues; their formal presentation detailed a history and current credit status that is fascinating. Here is a country that literally blew itself up in the course of 17 years of civil war, but it has never missed an interest or principal payment on what was, to Lebanon, a large combination of bank and sovereign debt. In addition to that presentation, Lebanese officials prepared a site on the World Wide Web, in English, containing updated economic and financial forecasts for the country. The lesson is that issuers can understand the importance of disclosure and high-quality information.

Another boost for disclosure will be the adoption of common international financial accounting standards. The move toward adoption has been slow to date but will likely accelerate as more crises occur and more market participants are drawn into solving those crises.

Even without international standards, the quality of accounting disclosure, particularly from the Latin American countries, has improved markedly since 1993; Mexican banks now use U.S. generally accepted accounting principles (GAAP), and Argentine GAAP standards are far more transparent and easier to understand than they were five years ago. This development reflects a willingness on the part of issuers to share data, which is based on the pragmatic realization that the external capital they desperately need follows ratings and ratings follow the availability of transparent and standard financial information. Another boost for improved disclosure has been the non-domestic-domiciled entities buying into the newly privatized businesses in many countries. Those entities demand adequate disclosure.

Analysts and portfolio managers must keep the pressure on, however, either directly on the governments or indirectly on the investment bankers selling the issues. The providers of information must understand that financial disclosure is vital to clients who do not have reserve positions that provide a comfortable exit strategy if issuers default. These investors' only real reassurance lies in the quality and quantity of information available at the time the investment decision is made.

The second basic tool in any sovereign analysis is political science. Outsiders can probably never capture all of the subtlety, all of the nuances, of an issuer's political environment, but analysts have to try because so much of what drives sovereign research is derived from the political framework of a country. Credit changes are as often, if not more often, the result of political forces as they are of economic or financial forces. If a government decrees, "There is now a moratorium on all debt payments," the investor is immediately in a workout scenario. So, the investor needs to know beforehand what the likelihood of such a decree is.

The political framework includes the form of government, the characteristics of the population and their actual or potential grievances, and the number and concerns of political parties and voter blocs. Particularly troublesome are substantial minority parties that can bolt the government in power at a moment's notice. Examples abound even in relatively developed countries, such as Hungary, Slovenia, and Yugoslavia. In these and other cases around the globe, population characteristics and ethnic rivalries could upset the timely payment of principal and interest.

The third tool for anticipating sovereign credit changes is macroeconomic analysis. What is the economic structure and extent of diversification within a country? What do the people do for a living, and how will they make money to pay investors back? The country's commodity and agricultural production is critical in some countries. Can the country feed itself? How important to a strong economy are exports? Exports are less important in some countries because their domestic economies are more vibrant than other countries'. I heard an analyst call Argentina "a basket case" because it does not export "enough." Argentina exports about 12 percent of its GDP, whereas Chile exports 24–26 percent of GDP. Neither country, however, can be defined as a basket case solely on the basis of export percentage. Argentina simply has a large, vibrant domestic economy that cannot be ignored.

The final element of macroeconomic analysis is the country's currency management and investors' evaluations of the currency. Is the country's currency stable and defensible, and will the country defend it? Currency maintenance has always been important, but it has come under the microscope since the summer of 1997.

Analysts should realize that currency management has an obvious dimension and a more subtle dimension. On the one hand, assessing currency management clearly involves determining the cost of supporting the value of a currency, which is determined by how much reserve spending the government would have to do to provide that support; that dimension has obvious inflationary overtones. More subtle, and probably more important, is the need for a country to maintain the currency at a certain level, or manipulate it to a certain level, to maintain competitiveness in export markets. It is critically important that the currency values of exporting countries be in sync with those of competing exporters. Many such countries (Venezuela being a prime example) make the mistake of letting their currencies appreciate against those of their principal competitors in exporting commodities or manufactured goods. The new "currency chemistry" that will arise out of Asia's totally destroyed currencies will be managed through various means—floating or fixed techniques—designed to maximize the competitiveness of the nations' manufactured products and other exports. The risk to this strategy is, of course, inflation.

The fourth tool in analyzing sovereign issuers and looking for potential changes in sovereign credit is analysis of banking-sector solvency. This factor has become even more important than in the past because of the recent examples of sovereigns assuming or guaranteeing the debt of the banks operating in their countries. Banking-sector solvency is a function of credit policies, bankruptcy laws, the existence and stance of supervisory bodies, and the quality of the accounting systems used to report bank performance. Several examples of past or current banking reform programs serve as previews of what will need to happen in many other countries. U.S. bank reforms followed the savings and loan crisis in 1990 and 1991. In 1995, the Mexican banks were reorganized, and Mexican officials, although they are still working at the task, have done a heroic job of putting back together a banking system that was in shambles. In 1997, many Thai banks were simply closed—admittedly, an extreme reform measure but one that was warranted under the circumstances.

The final tool for analyzing sovereign credit changes is a search for evidence that a country recognizes that economic and financial challenges exist and assurance that the country's recognition will turn into credible government policies and plans. Analysts and investors need to keep the heat on governments to continue to recognize and deal honestly with problems and to keep reminding them that their credit ratings and ability to issue sovereign debt are at stake.

Recent developments are heartening. A number of governments have had to impose tough new policies and make good on previous guarantees in order for various international organizations and other countries to provide support. In 1992, the Argentine convertibility program brought inflation down from dizzying levels to single digits. That change was an economic and financial miracle that gave Argentina the access to global capital markets that it did not have 10 years ago. For all the pain that austerity programs are causing in Brazil, the relatively stable currency under the Plan Real has meant great things for that country, which was torn by incredible inflation, corruption, and other social ills. The U.S. aid package to Mexico in 1995, despite criticisms as to the form it took, has worked. The United States has been paid back early and with interest, so the package was good for both countries. In Thailand, Thai leaders took the 1997 IMF program seriously and tried to address all of the IMF criticisms of their economy, their economic management, and their banking sector. The result is that Thailand's program for recovery is so credible that the country will likely be able to access the sovereign debt markets again relatively soon.

Conclusion

Because of the complexities and broad scope of sovereign credit analysis, and because of the exotic nature of many sovereign credits, sovereign credit analysis has an elegance that may have been "systematized" out of the analysis of many other investment sectors. The whole endeavor is as much art as science. Sovereign credit analysis has few hard-and-fast rules. If sovereign credit analysts and investors are insightful and ask the right questions, they will be able to accomplish the objectives that are common to investing in all sectors—developing an analytical framework, assisting in the evolution of capital markets, assessing relative value between issues and issuers, and constructing diversified portfolios without sacrificing an intolerable amount of return or adding an intolerable level of risk.

Question and Answer Session

George A. Ashur

Question: With all eyes currently on Asia, are some other parts of the world not receiving appropriate scrutiny?

Ashur: Absolutely. Some of the emerging markets of central Europe have problems brewing. Moreover, even though the developed European economies are doing better than they were a few years ago, implementation of the European Monetary Union will introduce a number of issues that many of us have yet to focus on. One challenge related to the new currency, which is going to be introduced in less than a year, will be what to do with the domestic debt that exists. The domestic debt of Belgium and of Italy, for example, is very large. What will such countries do without the ability to inflate their way out of debt problems as they have in the past? Another question is how the European central bank is going to function.

I also think that we have penalized some regions because of the fear that arose from the Asian problems. For instance, some of the Latin American countries have been unnecessarily penalized because of our fears about Asia.

Question: How does a country's decision to peg its currency to the U.S. dollar affect your credit analysis of that country?

Ashur: When a currency is pegged to the dollar, the biggest benefit is a decrease in inflation. So, in some cases, dollar pegs and currency boards are not beneficial. In other cases, they can have great economic improvement. Such a case is the convertibility program in Argentina, in which one-on-one exchange of the new peso for the dollar has meant a drop in inflation and which has been a terrific boon to that economy. That program permitted Argentina to grow at more than 8 percent in real terms in 1997 and brought the inflation rate down from more than 1,000 percent to less than 2 percent.

Question: How have the events in Asia affected your assessment of the risks in Japan, especially with respect to the Japanese banking sector?

Ashur: Unfortunately, the Asian crisis probably cannot be fully solved until we know the true nature of problems in Japan. Equally unfortunately, really knowing any Japanese sector is extremely difficult. The Japanese simply do not like to disclose information. Whether for cultural, historical, or operational reasons, the disclosures that we get from Japanese institutions are the worst in the developed markets and have been for decades. Are large Japanese corporations and banks hiding things that we need, and deserve, to know? We think they are. How do we get that information? I don't know. How do we assess risks in Japan and the outlook for the entire region without that information? Only tentatively at best.

Question: What sources do you rely on for political, cultural, and historical information about various countries?

Ashur: Sources for current news events range from English language news services that various countries have placed on the Internet to newsletters published monthly, weekly, or even daily by a number of political think tanks. In terms of cultural and historical insights, the best strategy is to read voraciously the widely available library sources; it is important for us to be literate about the countries in which we invest.

In terms of actually understanding a country and its culture, there is no substitute for visiting the country. I am not talking about a typical road show with an investment banker—staying at a luxury hotel downtown, being wined and dined by the minister of finance, and shaking hands with the president. You will get much more useful information by dressing down, walking around, seeing what people do for a living, seeing how they interact on a daily basis, and going into local restaurants and shops. The alert observer can pick up hundreds of useful insights into how the people live, work, and play. It is an intuitive process, as bottom up as it can get, but the kind of value you get from it can never be obtained from an office or a computer. The global village is a shopworn paradigm, but we are neighbors more than we ever have been before, and the best way to know your neighbors is to open the door and say hello.

EMU and the Bond Markets of Western Europe

Sean P. Flannery
Managing Director
State Street Global Advisors

> The creation of the European Monetary Union is one of the most momentous economic events of this century, with profound implications for the world's economy, bond markets, and indeed, capital markets in general. Although substantial risks remain with respect to the ultimate success of the EMU, the unification process is already bringing about changes that alter the complexion of investing in European fixed-income securities.

The pending establishment of the European Monetary Union (EMU) represents a paradigm shift for global bond investors and promises to affect everything from interest rates to business strategies, with changes resonating far beyond the physical boundaries of the union. This presentation provides an overview of the future steps in the unification process; discusses the impact of unification on the world economy, capital markets in general, and bond markets in particular; and identifies remaining risks that could threaten the unification process.

The Move toward Union

The movement toward monetary union in Europe has reached the critical period of implementation. The next major event occurs in May of 1998, when the official determination of the countries to be included in the first round of monetary union will be announced.[1] The initial union will contain 11 countries—Austria, Belgium, Finland, France, Germany, Ireland, Italy, Luxembourg, the Netherlands, Portugal, and Spain. Sweden, Denmark, and the United Kingdom have opted out of participation in the first round of EMU. Greece, the remaining European Union (EU) member, has not met the Maastricht Treaty criteria for joining the EMU.

The next milestone for the EMU will occur on New Year's Eve 1998, when "permanent and irrevocable" exchange rates vis-à-vis the euro will be established for all member countries' currencies. On January 1, 1999, those markets will adopt the euro and begin to trade, settle, and post income in euros. EMU sovereign debt will be issued in euros, and most other issuance is expected to follow suit. Most custodians—State Street Bank is an example—will begin to price in euros. These changes will mark the arrival of the first phase of implementation for the new currency.

Once exchange rates are fixed, clear-cut cross-currency relationships will exist: X amount in lira will equal Y amount in euros will equal Z amount in German marks, and so on. Other market changes will follow during the 1999–2001 period. For example, securities will be redenominated or renominalized in euros. Sovereign debt issues are expected to redenominate fairly quickly, perhaps immediately, into euros; private issuers will decide at their own discretion when to redenominate during the three-year period.

Although the economically difficult changes of the process will occur during the 1998–2001 period, the more emotionally difficult changes will come at the beginning of 2002, when the EMU begins issuing new euro coins and hard currency and retiring and withdrawing the member country or "legacy" currencies. Doubtless, the ultimate elimination of the legacy currencies on June 30, 2002, will prove difficult for some of the citizenry affected.

Impact on World Economy

The potential economic impact of the EMU bloc on the world economy becomes clear in comparing the size of the 11-country EMU with North America (the

---

[1] *Editor's note*: Some information in this presentation has been updated as of May 1998 by the author.

United States and Canada) and Japan. Using 1995 International Monetary Fund (IMF) data for relative GDP (measured in U.S. dollars), the economic comparison is as follows:

North America	38%
Japan	24
EMU 11	31
Non-EMU European Union	7

Measured by GDP, Europe (the EMU 11 plus the non-EMU EU countries) is roughly the same size as North America, and the EMU bloc alone is greater than Japan. Although the United Kingdom, representing about 6 percent of the 7 percent of the non-EMU EU bloc, currently holds a very strong position because of its relatively large position in the global bond markets, the emergence of the much larger EMU bloc could challenge that role. Given the United Kingdom's modest share in bond market capitalization under the euro regime, some see the U.K. bond market being pushed toward the sidelines. Monetary union in Europe could thus result in a sort of tri-polar regime with the United States, Japan, and the EMU as the dominant forces in the world bond markets.

The potential scale of the EMU bond market is difficult to gauge precisely, but some educated guesses are possible. One broad estimate used by the IMF is based on comparing debt securities as a percentage of GDP. Based on 1994 GDP (measured in U.S. dollars), the IMF estimates the following percentages of bond market debt (public and private) relative to GDP:

United States	152%
EMU 11	103
Non-EMU European Union	104

Using the U.S. percentage as the roughest of yardsticks, the EMU debt market could potentially experience growth in outstanding debt equal to roughly 50 percent of members' GDP. Even if debt does not rise to that level, the EMU clearly has enough room for a dramatic increase in issuance. As disintermediation takes place and corporations eschew bank financing in favor of going directly to the marketplace, public and private fixed-income issuance should begin to tap this unused capacity, causing this measure to rise.

Impact on Capital Markets

Historically, the European capital markets have not been particularly efficient. Certainly, one of the basic ideas behind monetary union is the desire to increase efficiency in the markets, in the forms of freer capital movement, elimination of currency risk, greater depth and liquidity, and disintermediation.

Free Movement of Capital. Investing in Europe in the past has been fraught with obstacles that made such investment much more difficult than in the United States. Capital should move more freely after implementation of the EMU because a single money market is likely to emerge. The region will have a single currency for settlement, similar trade and settlement structures, and beginning January 1, 1999, a new interbank system called TARGET that will facilitate settlements.

A key factor facilitating the free movement of capital will be the elimination under the EMU of artificial barriers that have proscribed and constrained capital movement. One of the largest barriers has been the currency-matching rule for insurance companies and pension funds that has long been in place in the EU. This rule demands that those investors match 80 percent of their assets to the currency of their liabilities. The shift to a single currency is likely to trigger an enormous reallocation of assets, particularly in asset-rich countries such as Germany. For example, German insurance companies will no longer be largely constrained to the German mark-denominated assets to support domestic liabilities; instead they can look across the EMU to find the most attractive assets with which to support the liabilities. The transformation of the liabilities to euros will expand the menu of assets to the entire unified zone. Removal of this barrier should have a large and salutary impact on the movement of capital throughout "Euroland," as some now call the zone.

By eliminating artificial barriers and enhancing capital mobility, the EMU will give domestic investors an opportunity to look beyond borders and take a pan-European approach to investing. Diversification also should be easier for investors when they are not so tightly restricted to their homelands.

Elimination of Currency Risk. Currency risk is usually the largest component of bond risk in international bond markets, so the elimination of currency risk within the EMU zone will mark an important change for bond investors. Every time an investor makes a decision to invest in bonds denominated in a foreign currency, the investor is also making a currency decision. Whether the investor takes on the currency risk, hedges it, or actively manages it, the investor has to make another decision. The elimination of currency risk within Euroland, then, will dramatically simplify the investment process.

As the EMU eliminates most currency risk, the evaluation of other risks, particularly credit risk, will increase in importance. Fortunately, the whole movement toward unification will increase pricing transparency and allow investors to more clearly compare bonds relative to the remaining dimensions of risk.

So, unification, via pricing transparency, should simplify the whole process of debt investing within the EMU bloc.

Market Depth and Liquidity. The broad-based framework that most of Europe will share under the EMU should cause European capital markets to grow deeper and more liquid over time. The broad euro base and increased cross-border flows—more money from more sources moving through different markets—should help insulate and provide stability to the capital markets. These benefits will be particularly important for the smaller countries, such as Portugal and Ireland, that do not enjoy easy access to the capital markets. Market liquidity will also be enhanced by the simplified trading that will follow the redenomination of securities into a single currency.

Another important aspect of increasing market depth and liquidity will be greater diversification of investment opportunities. With currency risk gone within Euroland, currency diversification will also disappear, so asset and market diversification will become more important. Investors in these bond markets will be looking for, and will be increasingly able to find, a wider variety of bonds to satisfy the increased need for diversification.

Disintermediation. In Europe, banks have traditionally dominated the credit scene. Borrowers, including municipalities, typically go to banks instead of the market, and all but the largest domestic corporations borrow almost exclusively from their own domestic banks. Traditions and practices between the European and U.S. markets have been dramatically different in this regard. Within the EMU bloc, for example, bank loans as a percentage of outstanding financial assets are about 57 percent, whereas in the United States, they are about 22 percent. European debt issuers were faced with the "anchoring" principle, which generally mandated that a domestic investment bank act as the lead on new bond issues and altered the complexion of the competition for new deals. As a result of the sometimes complex regulations related to debt issuance, market access for these issuers has been more difficult and less efficient for most European corporations than for their U.S. counterparts.

Implementation of the EMU should mean that banks will be competing on a pan-European basis. Some signs of that competition are already visible in the merger activity occurring on the commercial side. Over time, such activity should also materialize on the retail side as banks begin to compete for individual banking relationships throughout the zone.

The combination of a broader investor base and greater competition among investment bankers should lower the costs of gaining access to the markets. This substitution effect—that is, investors forsaking the banks to access the market directly to gain necessary financing—should lower the cost of capital for issuers. Thus, disintermediation brought about by the EMU will be an important factor in increasing market efficiency.

Impact on Bond Markets

The EMU, although not yet implemented, is already having at least three visible effects on global bond markets. First, the reaction to monetary union has, so far, indicated that market participants around the world are strongly confident that the EMU will occur—on time and largely as designed. Second, the countries themselves are getting fiscal religion. Third, the debt markets are indeed broadening and becoming more liquid.

Confidence in EMU. The best way to measure confidence is to see how the markets have been judging the expected effects of the EMU. The answer is, as **Figure 1** shows, that yields have converged steadily as the prospect of union has become more and more certain. The power of the convergence movement is dramatically illustrated in the spreads of formerly high-yielding countries, such as Spain and Italy. Smaller countries, such as Ireland, which have historically had to pay a premium because of illiquidity, have also benefited significantly from the sharp narrowing of spreads versus core credits, such as Germany. Other factors certainly contributed to this consolidation in yields—low inflation, fiscal discipline, and good liquidity in the markets—but bond investors have been betting for quite some time on the success of the EMU.

Fiscal Religion. Fiscal religion has become a global phenomenon: All around the world, countries are becoming more disciplined about managing their balance sheets and keeping their fiscal houses in order. The goal of meeting strict Maastricht Treaty criteria for membership may well have been the most important factor driving sovereign balance sheets among the EU countries. **Table 1** provides a snapshot of how the various EMU and non-EMU West European countries stood toward the end of 1997 relative to the Maastricht Treaty criteria.

The only country having trouble meeting the inflation criterion is Greece. Otherwise, the entire region is experiencing a relatively benign inflation environment largely because of fiscal conservatism.

The data for the deficit ratio tell a slightly differ-

Figure 1. Dramatic Yield Convergence

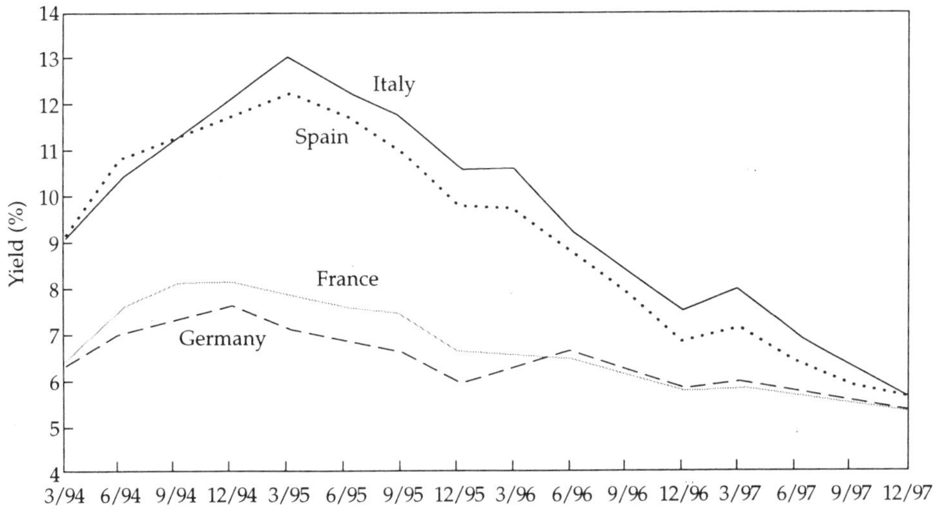

ent story: The general view is that, whereas most countries are beating the inflation criterion with room to spare, some countries (Italy, for example) will barely meet the deficit ratio criterion. A number of EMU watchers believe that "creative accounting," particularly by Italy and Germany, was used to meet these targets. Although these deficit ratios will change modestly before implementation of the EMU, all the countries except Greece apparently will meet this criterion. Whether the countries actually achieve this target now is less interesting, however, and certainly less challenging, than whether they can continue to do so over time. EMU naysayers tend to view the solid improvement in these measures as specious and are skeptical regarding the countries' ability to meet the criteria in the long term.

Many of the countries do not meet the debt ratio criterion at the moment, but most appear to be making progress toward meeting it. The countries' long-term interest rates are all close to one another—within about 40 basis points—and well under the established criterion, as indicated in Table 1.

Table 1. Meeting the Maastricht Criteria

Countries	Inflation: Less than Average of Lowest Three Members + 1.5%	Deficit Ratio (Government Deficit to GDP):[a] Less than 3%	Debt Ratio (Debt to GDP):[a] Less than 60%	Long-Term Interest Rate:[b] Lower than Average of Best Three Members + 1.5%
Initial EMU				
Austria	1.0%	–2.8%	66.1%	5.19%
Belgium	1.1	–2.6	127.4	5.17
Finland	1.9	–1.4	59.0	5.45
France	1.3	–3.1	57.3	5.05
Germany	1.9	–3.0	61.8	5.05
Ireland	1.6	0.6	65.8	5.33
Italy	1.5	–3.0	123.2	5.49
Luxembourg	1.3	1.6	6.7	5.39
Netherlands	2.5	–2.1	73.4	5.04
Portugal	2.2	–2.7	62.5	6.06
Spain	2.0	–2.9	68.1	5.30
Initial non-EMU				
Denmark	2.2	1.3	67.0	5.37
Greece	4.7	–4.2	109.3	—
Sweden	1.5	–1.9	77.4	5.54
United Kingdom	3.7	–2.0	52.9	6.11

[a]EU Commission 1997 forecast.
[b]10-year government bond yield on January 28, 1998.

Broader, More Liquid Markets. The extraordinary pace of sovereign issuance in Europe has eclipsed the broadening corporate debt market, masking the dramatic increase in both the size of the issues and the roster of issuers. Still, signs already indicate that the debt markets are becoming broader and more liquid. The evidence includes a nascent high-yield market in Europe, issuance of asset-backed securities, and more and more investor and issuer participation in the market. Three unresolved issues hold the key to how, and at what pace, EMU implementation will continue to affect the debt markets: the adoption of a benchmark for valuing debt securities, the evolution of a repurchase market, and the pace of non-sovereign-debt issuance.

■ *A Euroland benchmark.* One of the challenges for the EMU bond market is the lack of a central benchmark for comparison of bonds. In the United States, the "full faith and credit" Treasury market provides the framework for comparison of other credits that, by convention, are viewed as lower in credit quality. Euroland, however, has no such framework because it consists of 11 countries with varying degrees of creditworthiness. So, as those markets continue to develop, the question of who will win the benchmark race emerges. At least three strong candidates are apparent: the German yield curve, the French yield curve, and the euro swap curve.

From a fiscal standpoint, Germany probably has the best background for becoming the benchmark, and the German market is very large. The choice of Germany raises some liquidity issues, however, because the German yield curve exhibits spotty coverage with respect to the range of maturities available.

France, on the other hand, has broad exposure along the yield curve. In an effort to improve liquidity, France adopted a primary-dealer arrangement (similar to that of the United States) composed of about 20 primary dealers. France has also moved toward a more stable cycle of issuance, giving participants greater confidence in market liquidity. Unfortunately, the issue that always seems to haunt consideration of France as the benchmark turns on the question of credit quality.

Using a euro swap curve makes sense to many investment professionals. It is truly a market-driven rate, one that contains a generic, and relatively low, credit risk. On the other hand, some market participants are voicing a fair amount of dissatisfaction with this choice; they claim that the institutional presence of Germany or France is needed.

Good arguments can be made for each of the three possible benchmarks. Naturally, preferences sometimes have a nationalistic dimension. In reality, not one of the three is the perfect fit; each has some drawbacks as a potential benchmark. In this transition period, investors may have to look at all three spreads: to French rates, to German rates, and against the swap curve.

■ *A Euroland repo market.* The evolution of a centralized repurchase market will certainly have an important, and salutary, effect on debt issuance, but the establishment of such a market and how it will work are not yet determined.

One particularly important question for the functioning of the short end of the market is the relationship between the sovereign central banks and the European Central Bank. The current concept for repurchase agreements is that the national central banks will solicit bids in open market transactions, then feed the bids into a central facility for allocation. Ultimately, consolidated repo markets that function more like a single market should develop—featuring, for example, a fairly uniform short rate. Once a central market is established, it will simplify cross-border trade, provide a unified framework within Euroland for issuance, and facilitate more efficient financing of dealer positions. The expense and difficulty of such financing has been a hindrance to liquidity in continental Europe, where only France has enjoyed a well-developed repo market.

■ *Nonsovereign issuance.* Finally, and not surprisingly, the implementation of the EMU will spur nonsovereign issuance. This activity will give rise to a sharp change in the European debt markets of the future. Nonsovereign issuance will increase as bond investors' appetites cross all borders and as elimination of the matching rule opens a huge pool of assets to cross-border investors. In addition, credit ratings will no longer be capped by a sovereign credit rating. Furthermore, financing costs should fall as a result of the single-currency environment, in which most foreign exchange needs will be eliminated. In the long run, lower costs should lead to a decrease in spreads.

Increased underwriting competition should improve efficiencies in the issuance process and also enhance nonsovereign issuance. Competition to be lead underwriter on bond issues will be EMU-wide. Competitors will not need to have a subsidiary domiciled in the corporation's country (the so-called anchoring principle) in order to underwrite an issue. Historically, the European bond markets have been fractionalized, which is the result of stiff regulatory barriers, many small issues, and modest liquidity. We expect the fragmented nature of the market to change over time as both issuance and liquidity increase. One of the outgrowths of these markets, as national borders disappear, should be an increase in asset-backed securities (ABS). Different and perhaps disparate assets will be pooled, securitized, and sold as ABS, thus reducing the number of small issues in the marketplace and replacing them with a larger, more liquid issue.

Remaining Risks

So far, monetary union in Europe appears to be moving decisively toward becoming a reality. Even in the United States, where until recently few investment professionals other than bond analysts cared much about the EMU, attitudes seem to be changing. Investors are coming to terms with the fact that the EMU is a dramatic economic event, probably one of the most important in this century.

The success of the union appears to be assured right now, but numerous risks remain—some minor and several major. The EMU does not enjoy solid support in all of the constituent countries; legal challenges and other issues remain unresolved.

Delayed Implementation. First, many observers are concerned that a breakdown or delay in monetary union could occur—perhaps as a result of an upswell of nationalism, which should never be underestimated in Europe. History serves as an important guide to understanding the value Europeans have attached to their origins. It is hard to imagine a time in which the European economic or political climate was more charmed. Faced with the pain of a less friendly economic environment, more challenges to union might well arise, which, in turn, could threaten or delay the unification process.

Countries that have reaped the greatest benefit from convergence up to now, such as Italy and Spain, are likely to see dramatic widening of spreads if the unification process is derailed. Testament to these EMU-associated benefits is the fact that these countries' formerly higher-yielding sovereign credits have converged quickly to the German and French yield curves. Any delay would probably arrest or reverse that convergence.

Withdrawal. A second concern is that a country might withdraw from the EMU after entering. A country's withdrawal might be spurred by a dramatic change in political sentiment or a prolonged and adverse change in economic circumstances. Although, theoretically, a withdrawal is possible without destroying the EMU, the practical implications would likely be monumental. The costs to an individual country of joining the EMU are high, and many of the costs of establishing the EMU have been shared. Once foreign reserves are intermingled and national currencies eliminated, reversing those actions could be messy indeed. Many observers believe that if a major country were to withdraw from the EMU after its implementation, the whole system would fall apart.

Adverse Circumstances. Perhaps the greatest remaining uncertainty is how individual countries, or more importantly, the EMU itself, will weather the inevitable difficulties that will be encountered in continuing to maintain fiscal religion. Almost all the countries were able, by one means or another, to meet the Maastricht criteria by the deadline, but can they continue along that course? Tough fiscal decisions are coming up for many of the countries—Germany, Italy, and Spain—and their individual responses will obviously affect the EMU as a whole.

Fiscal Policy. Even more important is the sustainability of the EMU's unified fiscal policy. One key concern is the lack of clarity as to how economic policy will be carried out in a time of crisis. What are the responsibilities of the EMU, the European Central Bank, and the member central banks? In the event of a crisis, who would take what form of leadership and under what authority? Another threat to unified fiscal policy is potential wide divergence in national circumstances among EMU members. How would the union handle massive unemployment in one country, for example, or pressures for labor migration from a depressed national economy to a booming one, or one country's failure to address and contain its own economic problems? Answering these questions has proved to be difficult even among regions in the United States; the difficulty is potentially staggering in Europe, where language and nationalism are complicating factors.

Finally, the bottom line in assessing the likelihood of unified fiscal policy is the issue of how much tolerance for pain the Europeans have. In a positive economic and political environment, focusing on the efficiencies to be gained and on what has gone well in the EMU is easy. The true test will come when times are more difficult. What the EMU leaders and institutions do then will be the litmus test of the EMU's ability to function and prosper in the long term.

Conclusion

The creation and implementation of the EMU is an amazing confluence of events. The EMU represents one of the most important economic developments of this century. Optimism about its potential benefits understandably runs high, but pragmatism dictates that analysts recognize that the ultimate success of the union is far from assured. Expectations for a single bond market moving in lockstep are unrealistic; correlations will certainly increase, but spreads will continue to reflect concerns about credit quality and political issues. Nonetheless, the EMU's evolution is already fostering the critical ingredients of a dynamic bond sector—investor confidence, fiscal religion, and liquid and competitive markets.

Question and Answer Session
Sean P. Flannery

Question: Do you think trading of the euro initially will be strong or weak?

Flannery: We believe it will be fairly strong, albeit perhaps not dramatically so, and reasonably uneventful. One determinant of the euro's trading levels over time will be the appetite for the euro as a reserve currency, and some signs already point to sizable demand for the euro in that role.

Question: Do European sovereigns still offer any risk–reward opportunities, or has the time come to focus on European corporates?

Flannery: Given the convergence illustrated in Figure 1, sovereign spreads do not appear to offer much potential. We do not expect sovereign spreads to necessarily be static, however; some stretching and contracting over time, in response to political or economic situations, is likely. This instability could give rise to short-term spread opportunities. Some observers suggest that post-EMU European sovereign issues will evolve along the lines of debt issued by the Canadian provinces, which has been frequently characterized by spread volatility. Aside from those temporary sovereign spread differentials, however, European corporates will clearly offer the more attractive risk–reward profiles.

Question: Which groups or industries will have increased business risk because of reduced trade barriers and freer flows of capital?

Flannery: The banking sector should be significantly affected. A host of changes will make life more difficult for the banks—or at least for the marginal players. Some banks will lose their historical home court advantage, the number of players will probably increase, the breadth of the playing field will expand, and competition will stiffen. Furthermore, formerly captive domestic issuers can look anywhere they want within Euroland for the banking services they need. But keep in mind, some of the players will be well suited for this new environment and correctly positioned to profit from it.

More broadly, these changes may require investors to take a more global view, instead of focusing on country allocations, by comparing each company with its industrial peers around the world.

Eastern Europe

Ashwin Vasan
Vice President
OppenheimerFunds, Inc.

> Analyzing the large variety of East European debt securities and issuers is difficult indeed. The credits have the potential, however, to provide significant diversification benefits. Investors can tap that potential by understanding the tier system for East European dollar bond issuers and how local-currency bond markets in the region are likely to evolve.

The debt securities of Eastern Europe are probably the hardest in the world for which to perform credit analysis. The many countries vary so greatly—in history, culture, economic well-being, and future prospects—that analysts and investors may hardly know where to start. This presentation justifies the hard work required to analyze East European credits by enumerating the diversification benefits available and addressing the major issues in analyzing both sovereign dollar and local-currency fixed-income investments in the credit tiers of Eastern Europe.

Diversification Benefits

The East European fixed-income security market is characterized by two credit classes—a large group of high-quality, investment-grade credits and a smaller group of credits of very low quality issued by the transition economies, with all the associated risks. Within these broad credit classes, East European credits usually fit into one of the following three product categories, each offering potentially large diversification benefits.

- *Investment-grade sovereigns*. The sovereign immunity embedded in most sovereign debt covenants, with its attendant default implications, typically causes sovereign credits to trade at wider spreads than equivalently rated corporate credits. If investors do the credit analysis properly, they will find that the issuers of high-quality sovereign debt in Eastern Europe will typically have far more financial resources than issuers of investment-grade corporate bonds. Hence, high-quality East European credits have a role in dollar-based investment-grade bond funds—the role of providing investors potentially attractive arbitrage opportunities.

- *Low-quality sovereigns*. For investors who use the J.P. Morgan Emerging Markets Bond Index Plus (EMBI+) as a benchmark, Eastern Europe offers some of the highest yielding credits among the low-quality sovereign bonds that are available.[1] More importantly, these credits are a vital source of diversification in the EMBI+, which is 75 percent weighted in Latin America. Construction of the EMBI+ is based primarily on the bonds of countries that defaulted on their debts in the 1980s, and most of those defaults took place in Latin America. The EMBI+ is thus clearly not a diversified index from a mutual fund perspective, but all U.S. dollar-denominated emerging market debt indexes suffer from the same problem.

- *Local-currency debt*. For investors who use the global bond indexes as benchmarks, the local-currency-denominated bonds of Eastern Europe—particularly higher quality credits, such as Poland and Hungary—are an important source of diversification in indexes that, within about 12 months, will likely be weighted more than 50 percent in a single currency: the euro. To the extent that these East European markets will eventually develop local-currency bond markets, they represent the next convergence trade. That is, as Poland and Hungary move toward fixing their exchange rates to the euro, yields on Polish and Hungarian bonds will approach yields on euro-denominated bonds.

---

[1] The EMBI+ includes the Brady bond universe, Eurobonds, and some local-currency fixed-income loans. It was released in July 1995 with the series re-created from December 1993.

In short, Eastern Europe, unlike many regions of the world, has attractions for a broad spectrum of fixed-income investors, primarily because the market provides such a sharp demarcation between credits—a very-high-quality credit class and a very-low-quality class—and such a broad range of diversification benefits.

U.S. Dollar-Denominated Bonds

The East European sovereign credits can be divided into two tiers: the high-quality Tier 1 and the low-quality Tier 2.

Tier 1 Countries. A number of Tier 1 countries exist, and although their sovereign debt is all investment grade, a wide disparity of spreads exists among them. For example, of the five Tier 1 countries listed in **Table 1** (more countries exist in this tier than are listed; certain Baltic states, such as Lithuania and Slovenia, are excluded from Table 1 because they present no investment opportunities), spreads are as tight as 125–150 basis points (bps) above U.S. Treasury securities in the Czech Republic and Hungary and as wide as 375 bps for Croatia. Clearly, Croatia's spread reflects the continuing political risk that surrounds implementation of the Dayton Peace Accords.

The momentum, or potential direction, of these spreads is mixed. For example, in the cases of Poland and Hungary, the momentum is positive; that is, the potential exists for a credit upgrade and narrower spreads. In Poland, an accelerated privatization program is likely to result from election of the new government. Increased privatization is the last step needed in the Polish stabilization program to ensure the stability of the exchange rate regime and the movement of Poland's sovereign credit out of the low Baa3 rating up into the A spectrum. In the case of Hungary, the potential is for rising credit ratings following devaluation. Despite one or two slips (with respect to pension reforms), Hungary's economic policy has been exemplary.

In contrast, two countries for which the credit-rating momentum is clearly negative are the Czech Republic and the Slovak Republic. These countries share some interesting characteristics that will be familiar to those who have been following the meltdown in the Asian markets: weak banking systems, overvalued exchange rates, and most importantly, political paralysis on reform. Because these countries have economies in transition from state control to market economies, the people share no accepted wisdom as to who—the government, the people, businesses—should bear the inevitable costs and disruptions that privatization and the move to market mechanisms bring. That decision is a political one, so adequate political leadership is critical in these economies to bring about a transition that not only works economically but is also politically palatable, in the sense that the reforms have popular support.

■ *Political characteristics.* Because of the pace and magnitude of transition in so many of these countries, political aspects play a bigger role in Eastern Europe than in much of the rest of the world. Countries in the Tier 1 credit-rating group are characterized by, first, relatively advanced institutions of government. These countries have some checks and balances on government abuse of power and a tradition of the rule of law. When investors are relying on the representations and guarantees of counterparties in a country, the rule of law is enormously important, so transition economies with such political structures tend to attract foreign direct investment (FDI). The environment protects bondholder rights and can promote the creation of a corporate bond market—particularly in local-currency debt. Therefore, the evidence is strong that corporate bond markets will evolve in the Czech Republic, Hungary, and Poland.

In addition, a clear consensus has developed in the Tier 1 countries about economic policy. The favored policy, what might be called the Washington consensus (because that is where the International

Table 1. Selected Tier 1 Countries

Country	Credit Rating (Moody's Investors Service)	Spread over U.S. Treasury Securities (bps)	Credit Momentum
Croatia	Baa2	+375	Neutral
Czech Republic	Baa1	+150[b]	−
Hungary	Baa3	+125	+
Poland	Baa3	+200	+
Slovak Republic	Baa3[a]	NA	−

NA = not available.

[a]Negative credit watch.
[b]Approximate.

Monetary Fund and the World Bank have their headquarters), is one of low fiscal deficits, low inflation, privatization, and manageable current-account deficits. Consensus in the multilateral organizations favoring this policy for Latin America evolved in the 1980s, and it is clearly the policy imposed on the transition economies of Eastern Europe after the fall of the Berlin Wall. That this consensus has taken root is also clear in the political transitions that have taken place. For example, both Poland and Hungary have voted ex-communists back into power, but not only has market-oriented economic policy continued unchallenged, it has actually improved under the ex-communists.

Another interesting political characteristic of the Tier 1 countries is the role of their armed forces. The fact that the armed forces are under civilian control and, more importantly, that they view this control as appropriate for their role in society is critical because it reduces the threat of political instability. A positive by-product is that these Tier 1 counties have been offered membership in both the North Atlantic Treaty Organization, which is testimony to the West's belief in their institutional stability, and in the European Union, which is testimony to the fact that the West believes in their economic stability. Investors should pay close attention to which countries are accepted into NATO and the EU because such countries then become part of large organizations that have enormous vested interests in protecting their members.

Economic characteristics. The Tier 1 countries display economic fundamentals based on the Washington economic policy consensus. First, they have achieved macroeconomic stabilization. Fiscal deficits are small, inflation is in single digits, growth rates are high, public debt ratios are low, debt-service ratios are impressive, and foreign exchange reserve coverage is high.

Microeconomic stabilization is another matter. Privatization programs are in place, and despite occasional missteps, the pace of privatization suggests that the private sector dominates local economies and will be the primary engine of growth in those economies. Success of the privatization programs to date, however, seems to be related to whether the country pursued voucher privatization or the cash route. Most of the missteps occurred or are occurring in countries that went the voucher route; ownership was too widely distributed, which prevented knowledgeable shareholders from forcing company managers to improve their economic performance. Another microeconomic deficiency of these economies, one investors ought to pay attention to, is that they have no background or experience in corporate control, which hampers their ability to manage both the privatization process itself and the privatized entities that result. Poland and the Czech Republic are prime examples.

The Tier 1 economies tend to be light manufacturers. They are frequently viewed as manufacturing hubs for Europe, and their exports tend to be manufacturing, not commodity, exports, which differentiates these economies from many other developing regions.

The combination of political and economic stability has led to significant FDI in these countries. Hungary, Poland, and the Czech Republic, in that order, are the three largest recipients of FDI in Eastern Europe. (If the Russian privatization program ever gains momentum, Russia will be the largest recipient in the area of FDI flows.) The amount of FDI a country attracts is interesting from the perspective of how a country finances itself. Countries that receive FDI have a channel for funding in addition to portfolio flows or official bilateral or multilateral flows. The presence of FDI, especially given the recent experience in Asia, is a tremendous source of investor confidence because of the relative stability of FDI flows.

Tier 2 Countries. The sovereign debt of Tier 2 countries provides the most interesting market for EMBI+ investors because the credit ratings tend to be in the B range but the spread differentials are enormous, as can be seen in **Table 2**, and potentially represent opportunities for arbitrage. So, credit analysis for these debt issues has a role and does pay, especially given that the list of Tier 2 countries in Table 2 shows none with positive credit momentum.

Political characteristics. The political situations are not as clear in the Tier 2 countries as in the Tier 1 countries. The institutions of government are not developed. Checks and balances on government power are few. The rule of law is not firmly established. The issue of counterparty risk, which was so heavily tested in the aftermath of the Mexican devaluation and the current Asian devaluation, has yet to be tested in Eastern Europe, but the test will likely come soon.

Bondholders are greatly dependent on "good princes" to further their interests in these countries. In several Tier 2 countries, a handful of key people sitting in the central banks or finance ministries are responsible for solving very serious problems. In some cases, they are receiving financial support from the International Monetary Fund, but in a lot of cases, the IMF and other multilateral agencies are providing only advice.

Elections clearly show that consensus on economic reforms is absolutely nonexistent in Tier 2

Table 2. Tier 2 Countries

Country	Credit Rating (Moody's Investors Service)	Spread over U.S. Treasury Securities (bps)	Credit Momentum
Bulgaria	B2	+670	Neutral
Moldova	Ba2	+650	–
Romania	Ba3	+400	Neutral
Russia	Ba2[a]	+780	–
Turkey	B1	+400	–
Ukraine	B2	NA	–

NA = not available.
[a]Negative credit watch.

countries, and political transitions frequently throw the direction of reforms into question. Recent elections have presented stark choices in terms of how governments should be organized, although the distance between the extremes in electoral choices has narrowed somewhat. For example, in Russia, the choice between communism and capitalism has perhaps given way to a choice between a market democracy and crony capitalism.

The armed forces play an enormous political role in Tier 2 countries, which has important credit implications. For example, these Cold War armies are very difficult to dismantle, which affects fiscal deficits and national inflation rates. The countries in Tier 2 have not fully identified themselves, so regional conflicts—such as the conflict over Chechnya, the conflict between Turkey and Greece over Cyprus, and others that may develop from the minor skirmishes—will continue to be a factor in this region. Part of the reason is the mere presence of well-armed forces: Where power exists, it tends to get used, especially in countries with a tradition in which civilian authority frequently bows to the needs and desires of the military.

Economic characteristics. The economic characteristics of Tier 2 countries are troubling, to say the least. Macroeconomic stabilization is far from a reality. Fiscal deficits are large, inflation is high, and growth rates are negative. These countries are still paying for the pain and have not yet realized the benefits of transition, which has resulted in little popular support for reforms. Investors should not be surprised to see a backlash against the reform process and against implementation of the IMF and World Bank recommendations.

The public sector dominates the Tier 2 economies. Privatization is only beginning and is completely beholden to special interests. The attitude in these countries seems to be "I will let you privatize if you sell me the assets at a cheap price."

FDI is insignificant. Tier 2 countries are absolutely dependent on official flows to finance themselves. Export activity is dominated by commodities, primarily metals and oil. Therefore, the countries not only experience volatility in domestic macroeconomic variables (budgets, inflation, and growth), but volatility in commodity prices also creates macroeconomic instability in the external accounts. The balance-of-payments accounts are very vulnerable to what happens to oil and metal prices.

Russia. At Oppenheimer Funds, we believe that Russia, even though its debt is clearly one of the most volatile assets in the region and the country has one of the lowest ratings in the region, is the kingpin of Tier 2 credits and is, in fact, the key to Eastern Europe. Russia is a prime potential representative of the phenomenon known as contagion. Any instability in Russia will spill over into the rest of the region because of the sheer size of Russia and because failure of the IMF program in Russia will produce the loss of IMF credibility and have a significant impact on fixed exchange rate regimes throughout Eastern Europe. If the ruble goes, pressure will build on the other fixed currencies.

Russia faces problems with its budget, potential declines in commodity prices, and insufficient foreign exchange reserves. Russia just passed a 1998 budget that calls for an average interest rate of about 25 percent. But current market interest rates are about 40 percent. The budget targets tax revenues to rise by about 1.3 percent of GDP. But the history of Russian companies shows that they are notoriously unwilling taxpayers. Thus, investors should be very skeptical about the government's ability to raise tax revenues that meet the target.

With 85 percent of Russia's exports being commodities (oil and metals), any decline in commodity prices will have a substantial impact on budgetary revenues (to the tune of 0.3–0.5 percent of GDP) and the fiscal deficit. A price decline also will have an impact on the current-account deficit. If current price levels and commodity prices are sustained, Russia's current-account deficit will widen to 2.0–2.5 percent of GDP in 1999.

Finally, Russia's foreign exchange reserves are extremely low—about US$16 billion, or about US$18 billion if gold is included. Reserves are also low as measured in relation to imports and to foreign investment in the Russian treasury bill market.

Russia needs two things to stabilize itself and ensure that the ruble can continue in its present exchange rate regime: first, fiscal cuts of about 2 percent of GDP in order to merit a deficit target of 4.7 percent of GDP and, second, an enhancement of IMF support for the ruble through the Special Relief Fund, probably in the range of US$3 billion to US$5 billion.

Unresolved Credit Concerns

Clearly, the Washington consensus imposed on these countries a set of policies that are based on the experiences the IMF and World Bank have had in, primarily, Latin America. One credit concern in Eastern Europe stems from the fact that the Washington consensus does not address the issue of weak banking systems, and throughout Eastern Europe, whether in Tier 1 countries (Czech Republic, Poland) or Tier 2 countries (Russia, Romania, Bulgaria), the banking systems are extremely weak.

The use of fixed or quasi-fixed exchange rates to lower inflation, which is prevalent in these countries, creates a conflict—a race between the rate at which structural reforms can lower domestic costs and the rate at which the real exchange rate becomes overvalued.

In addition, many of these countries, especially in Tier 2, exhibit an excessive dependence on short-term financing provided by foreign investors. Russia stands out as an example: Foreign ownership of Russian treasury bills has varied from 30 percent to 60 percent.

Moreover, in few other heavily invested regions in the emerging markets is information of as poor quality as it is in Eastern Europe. This reality has implications: Investors in countries where information is poor typically arrive at overly optimistic conclusions and take overly aggressive positions. When reality finally hits them, the result is massive dislocations in the prices of financial assets as the investors all move in the same way at the same time.

Because the reforms imposed by the Washington consensus did not come to grips with the need for liability management of short-term debt and the need for restructuring of the banking sector, the next crisis the investment community will have to face may well occur in Eastern Europe. To explore this possibility, analysts need only consider what drove two major crises of the past two decades.

History Lessons. The Latin American crisis of the 1980s arose because of three factors, summarized in **Table 3**. First, the countries had extremely weak fiscal policies because they were basically following a model of development that dictated that Latin America build import-substituting industries, which are typically state owned, to advance industrial development. At some point in the future, the countries could then export the products of these industries. What happened was what usually happens with public investment: The rate of return on the investment was substantially below the rate of interest that was being charged on the funds used to build the industries. Consequently, the Latin American countries had to bankroll the industries. That financing came directly from their budgets.

Second, Latin America was greatly affected by a price shock to the oil producers in the region—Venezuela, Ecuador, and Mexico. Third, real exchange rates were tremendously affected by U.S. Federal Reserve policy and that policy's effect on the U.S. dollar. The greatest period of dollar instability coincided with the Latin America crisis. The influence on Latin America of the instability in the U.S. dollar in the 1980s is clear.

The current Asian crisis arose from somewhat different circumstances, summarized in the second column of Table 3. Fiscal policy in Asia was sound, and the countries of Asia were not commodity exporters. In fact, Asia is, for the most part, a region of manufactured exports. Dollar instability was not

Table 3. Factors in Credit Crises

Factor	Latin America in the 1980s	Asia in the 1990s	Eastern Europe Today
Fiscal policy	×		×
Commodity prices	×		×
Regional currency instability			
U.S. dollar	×		×
Japanese yen		×	
German mark			?
Weak banks		×	×
Fixed exchange rates		×	×
Short-term debt		×	×

an issue in Asia, but Japanese yen instability certainly was, and it was the first contributing factor to the current crisis. Exchange rate data indicate that the crisis coincided with the greatest period of volatility in the yen's real exchange rate since World War II. The three other major contributors to Asia's difficulties are familiar: the liability management of short-term debt, fixed exchange rates that had become increasingly overvalued, and incredibly weak banking systems. Investors and official institutions had several times asked the countries of Asia to change the fixed exchange rate regimes, but they refused to do so. The banking-system problems, especially in the case of South Korea, stemmed from financing policies in which governments chose to finance government initiatives through state banking systems rather than through fiscal accounts.

The Next Crisis: Eastern Europe? Eastern Europe has symptoms, shown in the last column of Table 3, of both the Latin American crisis and the Asian crisis. Fiscal policy in most of Eastern Europe, especially in the Tier 2 countries, is weak. Eastern Europe is extremely susceptible to commodity export prices, which also makes the region vulnerable to instability in certain currencies, especially the dollar. Yen instability is less of an issue, but German mark instability is an issue; the mark has not yet destabilized, but there is no guarantee that it will not. Banking systems in both tiers are weak. The entire region has fixed exchange rates; virtually all the currency regimes are peg systems of some sort. And short-term debt problems may be localized, but unfortunately for investors, they are localized in countries that hold the key to the whole region, such as Russia.

Local-Currency Debt

The attractiveness of any local-currency debt investment in Eastern Europe will be driven by two issues: correlation of the local-currency debt with sovereign dollar bonds and correlation of the local-currency debt with debt denominated in other local currencies.[2] East European domestic bond markets, especially in Tier 1 countries, should evolve relatively quickly over time because of four key factors that these countries exhibit:

- no history of high inflation, which inspires investor confidence;
- low public debt ratios, which clearly supports the issuance of long-term debt;
- open capital markets, which are critical for the development of local-currency markets; and
- external debts that are rated investment grade, which attracts foreign investors. Not only is a high debt rating a way to attract and develop interest in a local bond market, but it also means the countries have access to capital markets in periods of crisis. For example, in the aftermath of its devaluation, the Czech Republic was able to immediately raise an internationally syndicated bank loan of about US$1.5 billion to rebuild foreign reserves. Countries with non-investment-grade sovereign credits, such as Mexico, do not have that kind of access to capital markets after a devaluation.

Conclusion

Analyzing East European debt is difficult, time-consuming, and fraught with potentially insurmountable problems. The rewards of investing in this debt, however, are potentially great: large diversification benefits and attractive spreads. Analysts and investors who contemplate tapping East European credit markets, by way of sovereign dollar debt or local-currency bonds, will do well to recognize that the credits fall in different tiers in reflection of very real political, social, and economic differences among countries. Specific trouble in the future could come from the lack of liability management of short-term debt, weak banking sectors, and currency instability.

---

[2]For additional discussion of this topic, see *Global Bond Management* (Charlottesville, VA: AIMR, 1997).

Question and Answer Session

Ashwin Vasan

Question: What key factors would you look for to identify signs of a burgeoning crisis in Eastern Europe?

Vasan: Although people have spent their lives investigating so-called early-warning systems, no single system works. The signals we would have used based on the experience of Latin America in the 1980s would have led us completely astray in the 1990s Asian crisis. In fact, the reason so many investors got fooled by Asia may be precisely *because* they were following the signals of Latin America.

We have to look at a comprehensive set of signals, such as those summarized in Table 3. Unless we look at fiscal deficits, current-account balances, the actual and implied (resulting from the banking system) liabilities of the government, the posture of the corporate sector, and a whole host of other factors, we will not get a good idea of whether a crisis is brewing in the East European countries.

Question: In the context of a risk–reward trade-off, is buying Russian credits still warranted?

Vasan: For Oppenheimer Funds, this question involves the issue of portfolio construction. Russia is trading at 800 bps above U.S. Treasuries right now. The spread in that credit is enough for us to postpone taking an overweight position in Russia until we get a clear statement, from both the Russian government and the IMF, that the right set of policies is going to be pursued. The kind of rally that we are looking for in Russia, on the order of at least 200–300 bps, is not going to happen overnight, because the widening that has brought us to this point has taken six months or so to materialize.

Also, we use indexes as benchmarks and can take on only a limited amount of tracking error. If we are underweight in Russia and Russia is a large part of our benchmark, then we tend to be overweight in, for example, Poland because we prefer to have "contagion risk" rather than be invested in the source of the crisis.

Question: You mentioned that East European countries joining NATO and the EU would provide some measure of stability. The stability implied by South Korea's membership in global trading clubs and the Organization for Economic Cooperation and Development (OECD), however, was misleading. Would the stability you predict for Eastern Europe spring more from pulling the countries away from Russia than from economic integration in a larger entity?

Vasan: The integration of the countries into NATO and/or the EU would first have to be based on the countries meeting the organizations' standards, not application of different standards. In the example you mentioned, Korea, which is clearly deficient in providing investor information, was in an organization in which countries are required to provide such information. It is a mistake for an organization like the OECD to allow its membership to comprise two widely different sets of countries—one set that provides information and one that doesn't. After the debacle in Mexico, investors were asking how the funds and the financial markets could have missed the warning signs. The funds, in turn, wanted to know from the multilateral organizations why they invited into their clubs these countries, such as Mexico, that obviously did not disseminate transparent information. Transparent data ought to be a prerequisite before a country receives membership in the OECD or other multilateral organizations. Without that requirement, the financial markets are characterized by informational disequilibrium.

So, the membership of East European countries in NATO or the EU is not in the same category as Mexico or Korea in the OECD. Nor is it a case of weaning these countries from Russia. Joining the solid European clubs is a way of affecting domestic politics, a way of ensuring that the remaining fringe elements in domestic politics stay fringe elements. When these countries become parts of much larger organizations, they reach a point of no return in pursuing market-economy reforms.

Question: How do you integrate currency volatility in your management of East European credits?

Vasan: There is no one set of data, currency or otherwise, that helps in this regard. At the time of the Mexican devaluation, a number of economists on Wall Street were publishing reports stating that the exchange rate in Mexico was, at best, 10 percent overvalued. The same kind of analysis is currently being applied to Brazil. (The number 10 seems to be a magic number.) Asia was somewhat different because the Asian data indicated that the real exchange rates of Indonesia and Thailand were not overvalued. Unfortunately, that analysis prevailed because those countries displayed enormous productivity growth. So, what information is helpful? Clearly, current-account deficits matter. The profitability of key industries in the trade goods sector is another indicator of future currency volatility because what matters is whether people are making money or not and the profitability of the traded goods sector is what tells us whether real exchange rates matter or not. If companies have enormous flexibility on their cost side, and few of them anywhere in the world do, then it will show through in profits regardless of what is happening on the real-exchange-rate front.

Question: What is the outlook for credit growth in the region?

Vasan: Credit growth will follow improved credit quality. For credit quality in Eastern Europe to improve, a credit culture must develop and loans must be made. If the banks, which are designed to take on credit risk, are not taking on credit risk, they will take on other kinds of risks in their portfolios.

For instance, the Russian banking system is basically one big money market mutual fund that has no loans, and therefore, nothing affects the credit quality of its portfolio. But with the ruble forward contracts that they have written, which now total about US$17 billion, the Russian banks have transferred the credit risk that they ought to have taken into the foreign exchange market, which puts them at enormous risk if anything should happen to the ruble exchange rate. Low credit growth has often been argued to be a protection of the Russian banking system: The Russian central bank can raise interest rates to astronomical levels because it does not have to worry unduly about the impact on the domestic economy and on the banking system. What all the banks are doing is rolling over a stock of government debt; by definition, when the debt matures, it is valued at par, and the banks reinvest it at higher interest rates. Therefore, so the argument goes, high interest rates are actually good for the Russian banking system. But sooner or later, for an economy to grow, credit growth must occur, which happens only when banks act like banks and make quality loans.

Question: What kind of benchmark, if not the EMBI+, would be most appropriate for emerging market dollar bonds, both from Eastern Europe and from other regions?

Vasan: No appropriate benchmark exists; one has to be constructed. Some practitioners are working to construct better U.S. dollar-denominated emerging market bond indexes, so such an index should be available as an EMBI+ alternative in the future. The crisis in Asia may hasten the appearance of an appropriate index because the chances are that US$9 billion in debt will be issued by South Korea, maybe a few billion dollars by Thailand, and a few billion dollars by Indonesia, if that country gets its policy act together. The aggregate debt stock out of Asia will then be US$15 billion to US$20 billion, which suggests that the region should have a much higher index representation than its current 3 percent in the EMBI+.

Africa and the Middle East

David Larson
Vice President
Moody's Investors Service

> Africa and the Middle East, unlike other regions of the world, are not homogeneous regions that lend themselves to ready generalizations about country or bond market characteristics. Some countries are potentially attractive prospects for global bond investors, but the appeal of the region is limited by numerous factors, particularly a cloudy economic and political outlook.

Credit analysis in Africa and the Middle East is complicated because sensible generalizations are not possible about either the countries or their bond markets. Latin America, Eastern Europe, and Asia are fairly well-defined regions; for the countries grouped in one of these regions, analysts can generalize about the economies, characteristic patterns of development, and ways in which shared cultures and histories influence political, legal, and even corporate structures. In the Africa/Middle East region, some 80 countries are lumped together under a heading that might most honestly read "Rest of the World." This presentation first offers a few broad observations that apply in a majority of cases, then provides more specific analysis of nine countries assigned credit ratings by Moody's Investors Service.

Regional Background

The economies of Africa and the Middle East (defined broadly to include Turkey and Pakistan) have tended to be resource based and reliant on exports of primary goods to the developed world. Today, perhaps the most striking characteristic is the low level of integration of these economies with the global economy: The share of Africa and the Middle East in total world trade is both very small and declining—from 6.7 percent in 1990 to 5.5 percent in 1996. Net capital flows to this region lag far behind the flows into other regions.

Some hopeful signs of change are visible, however. Most governments in Africa and the Middle East now accept the need for market-oriented policies. Even the African countries of Uganda and Côte d'Ivoire show some stirrings of economic life.

Only a handful of countries have come far enough, however, to become participants in bond markets. As shown in **Table 1**, Moody's ratings list shows only 13 countries in the Middle East and North Africa and only one country in Africa below the Sahara (the Republic of South Africa) with ratings, or country ceilings. Moreover, many of these countries are not bond issuers; Moody's has assigned such countries ceilings because it is interested in rating the banks domiciled there. In the mid-1990s, however, Turkey was the only country in the entire region with a rating, so the trend suggests that the number of countries in the region with ratings will likely increase in the next two years; perhaps two or three more countries from the Middle East and another four or five from Africa will be rated.

Despite the sleepiness of the region in general, some countries have already tapped international capital markets for bond financing and others have the potential and the incentive to do so in the near future. In particular, three individual countries and the six Arab Gulf countries that constitute a subregion comprise identifiable pockets of interest for bond investors and present some intriguing challenges for the credit analyst.

Turkey, South Africa, and Israel

The three countries in the region that are likely to hold the greatest interest for bond investors are Turkey, South Africa, and Israel. This section analyzes what Moody's regards as the critical issues for these countries' economies and creditworthiness.

Turkey. Turkey is by far the most active issuer of foreign currency bonds in the region; by itself, Turkey accounts for roughly half of total Eurobond

Table 1. Moody's Country Ceilings

Country	Bonds/Notes	Bank Deposits
United Arab Emirates	A2	A2
Israel	A3	A3
Kuwait	Baa1	Baa1
Oman	Baa2	Baa2
Qatar	Baa2	Baa2
Saudi Arabia	Baa3	Baa3
South Africa	Baa3	Ba1
Tunisia	Baa3	Ba1
Bahrain	Ba1	Ba2/A3
Egypt	Ba1	Ba2
Jordan	Ba3	B1
Lebanon	B1	B2
Turkey	B1	B2
Pakistan	B2	B3

issuance in Africa and the Middle East. Turkey first approached the market in 1992, and it now has nearly US$15 billion in foreign currency bonds outstanding, which is more than 30 percent of the government's cross-border debt. Turkey also has a sizable domestic treasury bill market, with substantial foreign participation attracted by real interest rates of up to 25 percent.

Returns of that size imply a high level of risk, and the economic data in **Table 2** confirm that implication: Large budget deficits have led to chronic high inflation (estimated for 1997 at nearly 100 percent), but economic growth has been strong, which confirms suspicions that the authorities have done essentially nothing to counter inflationary pressures in the economy. This situation is inherently unstable. Indeed, the data for 1994 reflect a run on the Turkish lira in January that forced the government to raise interest rates as high as 400 percent while carrying out an abrupt tightening of fiscal policy. The result was a 5.5 percent one-year fall in GDP.

The paradox of Turkey is that the real economy, excluding the 1994 debacle, has been doing well in spite of poor economic policy and an unstable macroeconomic environment. The private sector has proved its resilience and dynamism by flourishing in these difficult conditions, which is a testament to the enduring success of the economic reforms of the 1980s carried out under the leadership of the late Turgut Ozal. He oversaw the transformation of the economy from a highly regulated, import-substituting regime to an open, liberalized, and export-oriented regime. This change has had two important consequences: First, Turkey has experienced the emergence of strong, internationally competitive companies that are able to deploy economic resources far more efficiently than either the private sector of two decades ago or the public-enterprise sector of today. Second, deregulation and price liberalization have enabled the economy to adjust rapidly to changed circumstances. As a result, the economy is able to perform far better than might be expected in a dangerously unstable environment.

This real economic performance helps explain the reasonably healthy condition of Turkey's external accounts. A floating, market-determined exchange rate ensures that importers and exporters generally do not respond to distorted price signals. Even after three years of inflationary, demand-led growth, the current-account deficit is still relatively modest. Similarly, Turkey's foreign debt burden is not exceptionally onerous, certainly not for a B1-rated country.

Despite these undeniable strengths, Moody's assigns Turkey a low country ceiling because of the development of adverse economic policies since the early 1990s and the related political risk. From a bond-rating perspective, the most remarkable fact about Turkey's brief history as a foreign bond issuer is that in six years, the country has gone down four notches in credit rating—from an investment-grade rating of Baa3 to a B1 rating, the same level as Brazil. Most of the downgrading occurred during the 1994 currency crisis, but Moody's and the other agencies have since then lowered the rating again.

The experience of the 1994 crisis was crucial in this regard: Before that crisis, Turkey could be viewed as an economy with a successful but incomplete reform program. Fiscal policy was dangerously loose,

Table 2. Turkey: Country Ceiling—B1

Economic Indicators	1993	1994	1995	1996	1997E	1998F
GDP growth rate	8.0%	–5.5%	7.2%	7.2%	6.0%	4.0%
General government balance/GDP	–6.8	–4.4	–4.4	–8.5	–9.4	–8.5
Consumer price inflation	66.1	106.3	88.1	80.3	95.0	75.0
Current account/GDP	–3.6	2.0	–1.4	–2.4	–2.3	–2.5
Foreign currency debt/GDP	32.2	48.0	40.8	41.0	40.3	40.1
Foreign currency debt/exports	185.9	189.0	162.1	154.3	155.4	150.0
Debt-service ratio	26.4	30.1	27.3	22.3	27.2	27.4

E = estimate.
F = forecast.

and privatization was stalled. Many analysts assumed that a government that had already done so much to open the private sector would sooner or later put the public sector right. Most important was the assumption that the authorities would act as soon as the economy was in danger. These assumptions proved to be wrong. Even after the crisis hit, the authorities responded only with short-term emergency measures. The underlying problems of fiscal policy that led to the crisis were not addressed, and they have worsened as a result.

Moreover, the Turkish political situation has been in more or less constant turmoil since about 1994. Government control has changed four times since the end of 1995, and the most recent change, in June 1997, was directly attributable to pressure from the military. The Constitutional Court recently outlawed the Welfare Party, an Islamist political party that won the largest share of the vote in the last general election. The present government is a minority coalition of one center-left and two center-right parties that relies on the support of a small left-wing party to stay in power. These conditions are not likely to produce the necessary bold and painful economic reforms. If Turkey ever gets policy right, however, bond investors are likely to see rapid improvement in the country's economic outlook.

South Africa. Of the approximately US$8 billion in South African cross-border bonds outstanding, nearly all were issued by the Republic of South Africa or other public-sector entities. The domestic bond market is far larger than the foreign bond market, more than US$70 billion, with most issuance again by the government or several large public corporations. In the past few years, a Euro-rand market has emerged, so total foreign bond issuance includes about US$5 billion of rand-denominated bonds. In fact, because of capital controls, offshore rand instruments are indexed only to the rand exchange rate and are settled in foreign currency.

The issue of capital controls is central to Moody's view of South Africa. These controls are a relic of the last decade of the apartheid regime, when the government announced a moratorium on short-term debt repayments, created a two-tier exchange rate system, and placed stringent restrictions on capital-account transactions. These measures began as emergency policies for dealing with capital flight at a time of political crisis. Since the peaceful transition to nonracial democracy, the authorities have unified the exchange rate and partially freed capital-account activities. Substantial limitations remain, however, particularly on outward investment. The limits are understandable; the rand fell nearly 30 percent against the dollar in 1996, and for most of the 1990s, official reserves have been quite low, averaging less than one month of import cover. Moreover, the central bank has little scope for tightening monetary policy. As shown in **Table 3**, GDP growth, following a long recession, has recovered only moderately.

The situation in South Africa is difficult but not hopeless. Moreover, a strong case can be made that capital controls are discouraging stronger capital inflows more than they are blocking outflows. Certainly, many billions of dollars have left the country illegally since 1985 despite the controls, and pent-up demand for overseas assets may have dwindled to nothing. If so, then the central bank can reasonably hope that gradual liberalization will strengthen the balance of payments. Evidence exists that this process has indeed already begun. Since the lifting in 1997 of a number of restrictions on domestic banks' overseas investment, South Africa has experienced strong net capital inflow. By year end, reserves were at about US$5 billion, more than two months' import coverage and the highest level in many years. Markets may have interpreted the liberalization as a sign of confidence; at a minimum, it was obviously not the signal for a large-scale movement of funds out of the country.

Moody's outlook for South Africa's Baa3 rating was negative in early 1997 because of concern over continued pressure on the currency and weak international liquidity. So far, however, the investment-grade

Table 3. South Africa: Country Ceiling—Baa3

Economic Indicators	1993	1994	1995	1996	1997E	1998F
GDP growth rate	1.3%	2.7%	3.4%	3.1%	1.7%	2.7%
General government balance/GDP	−8.2	−9.2	−5.7	−5.4	−5.5	−4.5
Consumer price inflation	9.7	9.0	8.7	7.4	8.8	7.5
Current account/GDP	1.6	−0.3	−2.1	−1.6	−1.0	−1.0
Foreign currency debt/GDP	14.8	15.3	16.8	20.3	21.4	21.6
Foreign currency debt/exports	60.7	62.0	65.7	75.1	74.4	71.4
Debt-service ratio	13.1	12.7	11.9	7.4	8.3	7.6

E = estimate.
F = forecast.

rating has held because of the many countervailing strengths of the economy. First, as the data in Table 3 make clear, South Africa is a lightly indebted country. Standards of accounting and disclosure are high, so bond investors can be confident that a crisis will not bring to light additional billions of dollars of debt. The political situation is good, although the crime situation is not. The government enjoys broad support and will not face serious opposition in next year's election. And the government is drawing on that support to maintain an economic policy framework that is, on the whole, prudent and market friendly. Fiscal policy has been tightened despite enormous pressure on the government to do more to address wide income disparities and make up for years of underinvestment in the nonwhite communities. Even privatization, which has been anathema to organized labor, is being pursued with some vigor.

The greatest economic challenge for South Africa will be to find employment opportunities for its jobless population. The overall unemployment rate is an almost unbelievable 30 percent, and the rate is even higher among poor blacks. Perversely, government labor policies are likely to make the situation worse. A more restrictive Conditions of Employment law and higher minimum wages are almost certain to limit job growth. Organized labor was a loyal supporter of the now ruling African National Congress during the apartheid era, so political considerations make any change of direction on these issues difficult for the government. Eventually, however, a more flexible labor market will be essential if South Africa is to have any hope of making inroads against unemployment.

Israel. Israel has issued a large number of foreign currency bonds, but US$9 billion of these securities carry a U.S. government guarantee as part of a housing loan program designed to help deal with an influx to Israel of immigrants from the former Soviet Union. An additional US$8 billion is in the form of Israel Bonds, unrated, nonmarketable instruments generally bought by overseas supporters of Israel. The Israeli government first entered the Eurobond market in its own name in 1995 and, today, has a total of about US$1.5 billion in bonds outstanding, including some issued by the publicly owned Israel Electric Corporation. Israel also has an active domestic government bond market with US$39 billion in bonds outstanding, most of which are linked to either inflation or currency. The government introduced these indexed instruments in the early 1980s, when Israel was suffering from very high and accelerating inflation.

A stabilization program introduced in 1985 began a wholesale transformation of Israel's economy. Although incomplete, the process of stabilization has helped Israel develop into a modern free-market economy. Exports, which were once dominated by agricultural products, are now led by a flourishing high-technology sector—in particular, sophisticated electronics and software. Public expenditures and indebtedness have fallen sharply from their levels in 1985. Of equal importance, the government has withdrawn from the central role it formerly played in the real economy: Most subsidies and directed lending have been ended, and privatization has begun in earnest. In 1997, privatization revenues came to more than US$4 billion.

The size and terms of the government's domestic bond issuance have effectively blocked the emergence of a corporate bond market. In the near future, however, the best private-sector entities are likely to begin tapping the Eurobond market, just as many of them have entered overseas equity markets.

Persistent high inflation, however, is evidence that the transformation process is incomplete. As **Table 4** shows, inflation in Israel, although far below the 500 percent rate briefly reached in 1985, is still excessive by developed country standards. Nevertheless, in 1997, inflation fell to 7 percent, the lowest rate in 29 years, which is surely an encouraging sign. This improvement was achieved by means of extremely tight monetary policy, however, and fiscal

Table 4. Israel: Country Ceiling—A3

Economic Indicators	1993	1994	1995	1996	1997E	1998F
GDP growth rate	3.5%	6.8%	7.1%	4.4%	2.1%	2.5%
General government balance/GDP	–3.9	–2.1	–4.1	–4.7	–2.4	–2.4
Consumer price inflation	11.2	14.5	8.1	10.6	7.0	6.5
Current account/GDP	–2.7	–3.4	–5.5	–5.6	–3.7	–4.1
Foreign currency debt/GDP	40.3	36.0	34.9	32.3	40.6	42.2
Foreign currency debt/exports	87.7	83.7	81.9	79.5	97.8	99.6
Debt-service ratio	14.7	15.3	15.1	15.7	14.3	14.7

E = estimate.
F = forecast.

austerity, aided by an appreciating currency. The price paid for this improvement included the slowest economic growth of this decade for the country and rising unemployment. Making sustainable progress against inflation will require increased deregulation and liberalization, particularly of the capital and labor markets.

Moody's rating for Israel of A3 is constrained by considerations of political and security risks. Because these factors are already built into the rating, however, the A3 should survive a fair amount of bad news; that rating is certainly not based, for instance, on benign assumptions about the future of the peace process. In any case, most of the real economic benefits of the peace process have already been captured. The end of the Arab League's secondary boycott has given Israel access to significant new markets for trade and investment, especially in Asia, and a reversal of those gains is almost inconceivable. At the same time, even a full formal peace with its neighbors under the terms of the Oslo accords would not eliminate the need for Israel to maintain a strong—and expensive—military establishment.

To a certain extent, internal political considerations are also a limiting factor on raising Israel's credit rating. Reaching an accommodation with the two million Palestinians living in the Occupied Territories will be long and arduous. It will inevitably be accompanied by periodic episodes of violence, which always carry the risk of a more serious deterioration of public order and security. Moreover, the many divisions within Israeli society are reflected in politics: 13 parties are represented in the 120-seat legislature, and 7 of them belong to the governing coalition. The parties' competing claims constitute a permanent threat to the development of prudent economic policies.

On balance, Israel's prospects appear bright, with the economy well-positioned to take advantage of the country's well-educated work force.

The Arab Gulf Countries

The six Arab Gulf countries that make up the Gulf Cooperation Council (Saudi Arabia, Kuwait, the United Arab Emirates, Bahrain, Qatar, and Oman) constitute a subregion with intriguing challenges for the credit analyst. Moody's has published country ceilings for these members of the Gulf Cooperation Council (GCC) since January 1996. Of the six, only Qatar and Oman have been involved directly or indirectly in foreign currency bond issuance. But with oil revenues stagnant at best, these countries are looking increasingly like potential customers for the global capital markets, and greater bond issuance in the future is highly probable, especially as an element of project finance.

The current spread of country ceilings for the GCC countries is not great—from A2 at the top end to Ba1 at the other (see Table 1). This small range should not be surprising in light of the features common to all these countries: an economic reliance on oil and gas exports; similar political regimes, demographic profiles, and fiscal arrangements; and a shared security environment. Important differences do exist among the countries, however, which Moody's has tried to capture in the ratings. This section examines the countries within the context of those key differences, beginning with issues related to the Gulf's energy resources.

Oil Market Outlook. Energy is obviously the most important factor in the Gulf economies. Oil and gas account for more than 90 percent of export receipts and 80 percent of budget revenues, and the totals are so large that in less than a generation, the GCC governments have been able to build modern physical infrastructures and provide their citizens with the most generous social welfare systems in the world.

Reserves and production. The six countries are not equally endowed, of course, with oil and gas resources. In terms of crude oil reserves, Saudi Arabia is preeminent, but the United Arab Emirates (UAE) and Kuwait also have enormous reserves. These three account for about 45 percent of proven world reserves of oil. Qatar and Oman have significant quantities of oil; Bahrain's reserves are small and declining. The picture for natural gas is somewhat different: Qatar is in first place, followed by the UAE and Saudi Arabia. Again, Bahrain's reserves are the least substantial.

What matters most for credit analysis is production—the rate at which these reserves are converted into financial flows. Each country's annual production of oil and gas is shown in **Table 5**. Production levels show the same ranking as for crude oil reserves but with a narrower range. For example, Saudi Arabia's total output is only about 40 times that of Bahrain, even though Saudi Arabia's reserves are more than 1,000 times larger. Of course, Saudi Arabia will be able to sustain production longer (at least 100 years at current rates), but that is far beyond the 7 to 10 years we consider in assigning a long-term rating.

Reserves and production rates can be important as an indicator of the potential for future increases in production. In Qatar, both oil and liquefied natural gas (LNG) output are growing significantly, whereas the low level of reserves in Bahrain implies that production is likely to decline in the near term. The three largest producers, however—Saudi Arabia in particular—are constrained by the very size of their current output. They cannot pump substantially more oil without putting downward pressure on prices; thus, they have limited scope for increasing their revenues.

Table 5. GCC Production of Crude Oil and Natural Gas, 1996

Country	Production (million tons and equivalent)	Production per Capita (tons and equivalent)
Saudi Arabia	466.0	NA
UAE	148.8	63.6
Kuwait	112.6	64.3
Oman	47.9	21.8
Quatar	34.0	55.7
Bahrain	11.1	18.2

NA = not available.

Further refinement can be made to this analysis of each country's relative oil wealth. The last column of Table 5 shows (as available for 1996) each country's total oil and gas output divided by the country's population, which gives a better idea than pure production levels of the scale of a country's income relative to the population-induced demands that will be placed on that income. With this measure, the six GCC states fall into two groups, with the low-population, high-resource countries of Kuwait, the UAE, and Qatar well ahead of Oman and Bahrain (and using 1995 data, Saudi Arabia).

Prices. The second key element of any oil market outlook is pricing, and **Figure 1** shows that oil and gas prices, as reflected in the Brent crude complex,[1] have generally weakened, both nominally and in constant dollars, since 1980. Note that the oil price collapse—the third oil shock—occurred more than 10 years ago and has long since been absorbed by the market. The Arab Gulf states built their infrastructures and set up their systems of social welfare largely before 1985. The costs of basic infrastructure had been mostly paid by the time oil prices fell, so much of the initial adjustment to lower prices could be achieved by reducing public investment spending. In contrast, social spending—free housing, education, and medicine; guaranteed employment; virtually free public services—was never affected, and prices are not likely to rise by enough to spare governments the need for such adjustment.

Growth in world demand for oil and gas should permit a moderate increase in volume and prices, but any sharp increase in prices will probably elicit a supply response strong enough to reverse the effects. In real terms, after all, even 1997's average price was no higher than in 1987. For the foreseeable future, then, investors can assume that *on average* the major oil producing countries will experience only small incremental growth of their export revenues.

---

[1] The Brent crude complex, used to price two-thirds of the world's internationally traded oil, consists of three related markets: dated or physical Brent, forward Brent, and Brent futures.

Figure 1. Brent Crude Oil Spot Prices, 1980–97

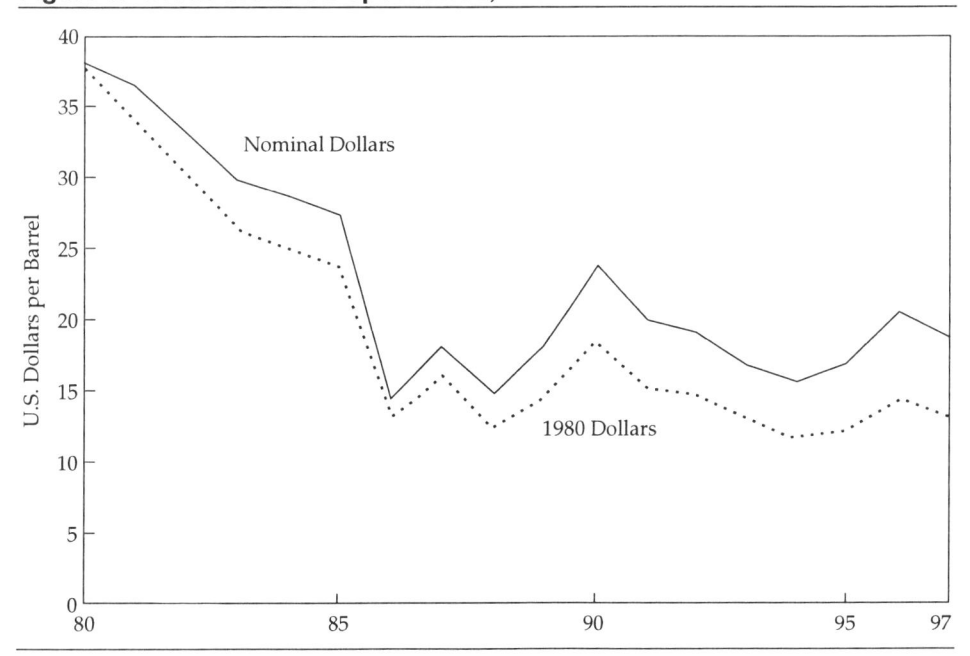

Fiscal Policy. Oil and gas production support the credit ratings of the GCC countries, but certain factors limit the rating ceilings. Limiting factors are typically external constraints, such as a weak current-account position or a large stock of foreign debt, but in the case of the GCC countries, the limiting factor is fiscal. **Figure 2** allows comparison of the external balance and the fiscal balance for each country. It shows the cumulative current-account balances and budget balances of the most recent five years divided by the country's 1997 GDP. In four instances, the current-account position is clearly stronger than the fiscal position; in fact, Kuwait and the UAE have had current-account surpluses averaging 10 percent of GDP. Of the two exceptions, Qatar's current-account deficit is the result of heavy import requirements for that country's LNG projects, and the current account should return to a wide surplus in three to four years as those projects are completed and placed in production. Saudi Arabia's current-account deficit, however, is structural; it reflects the high absolute level of import demand from a much larger population than in Qatar.

The fiscal deficits have their origin in the period of high oil prices, when GCC governments built up high levels of current expenditures financed entirely from budgetary oil revenues. Even before 1985, a number of the countries, including Saudi Arabia, were beginning to experience budget shortfalls, but deficits widened considerably thereafter. The problem has two aspects: First, governments have been reluctant to limit the growth of social expenditures, and second, even as oil revenues stagnated, the governments were equally hesitant to seek alternative sources of revenue.

Saudi Arabia's experience provides a typical example of the second point. Some growth has occurred in nonoil revenues, especially since 1994, when many public-service charges were raised. Even so, budget outcomes still depend overwhelmingly on oil revenues. For example, 80 percent of the improvement in the Saudi budget deficit since 1994 has been the result of higher oil prices. In fact, nonoil revenues as a percentage of total revenues were actually slightly lower in 1996 than in 1989. Several GCC countries have managed to raise the share of nonoil revenues in this period, but only Bahrain has done so significantly.

Oil revenues are not a form of tax income; rather, they are typically the proceeds of the national oil company's own operations. In effect, nonoil revenues represent the total tax-raising effort of the government (broadly defined, of course, because such revenues include user fees and other charges not usually regarded as taxation). **Figure 3** shows nonoil revenues as a percentage of GDP (a common measure of tax-raising effort) for Bahrain, Kuwait, and Saudi Arabia and illustrates two key points with respect to

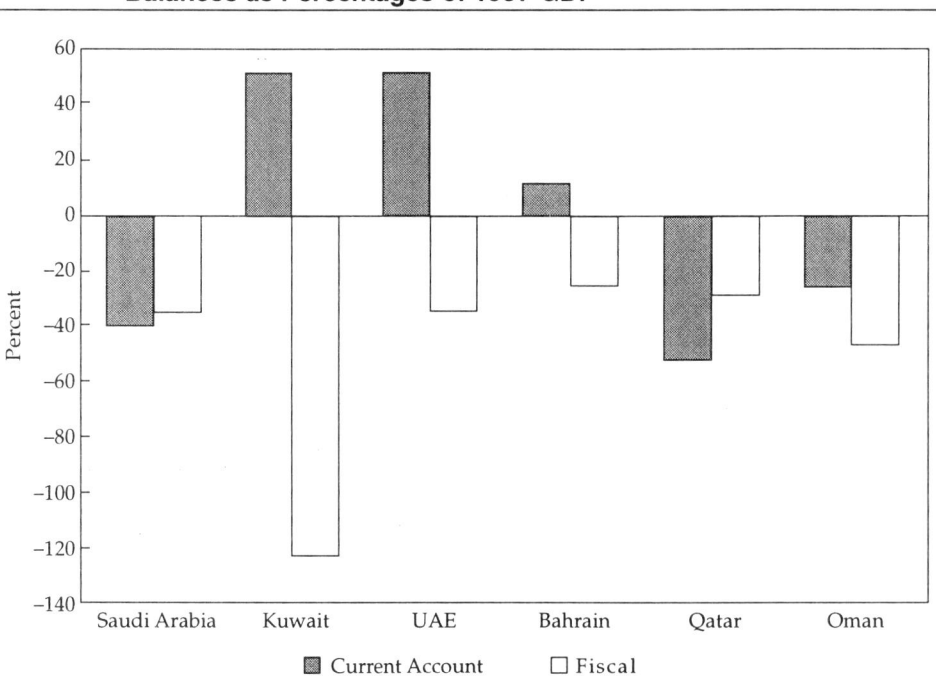

Figure 2. Cumulative 1992–97 Current-Account Balances and Fiscal Balances as Percentages of 1997 GDP

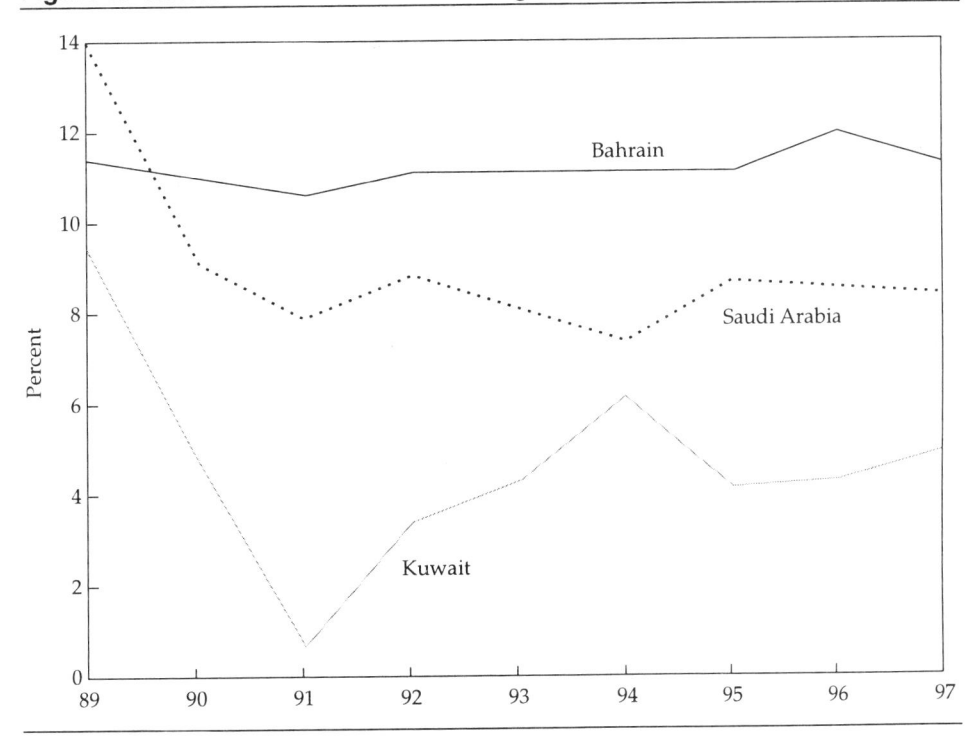

Figure 3. Nonoil Revenues as Percentages of GDP, 1989–97

nonoil revenues. The first point is that no clear trend emerges in the 1989–97 period. The second point is that even Bahrain's nonoil revenues come to no more than 12 percent of GDP; for the rest of the GCC, nonoil revenues are considerably less.

Expenditure data reveal a somewhat different picture. Some of the GCC states have achieved substantial reductions in spending relative to GDP since the mid-1980s. The Saudi government, in particular, has made a sustained effort to rationalize expenditures—by, for example, sharply reducing its program of agricultural subsidies (which at one point guaranteed wheat growers a price nearly 10 times the world market price). In nearly all cases, capital expenditures have been reduced by almost half in Saudi Arabia.

Current expenditures remain under strong upward pressure, and future efforts to cut or restrain expenditures will have to focus on what can be termed "social expenditures"—the lavish spending on their own populations that the GCC governments have traditionally used to channel oil wealth from the public to the private sector.

The difficulty today is that governments are spending more than their oil wealth is bringing in, a fact confirmed by the gap between the current-account balances and fiscal balances. In most cases, budget deficits have been financed by drawing down official foreign assets, which represent accumulated past oil wealth. One exception is Saudi Arabia, which has apparently made little use of its foreign assets since the Gulf War. Instead, Saudi Arabia has financed budget deficits primarily with domestic debt; as a result, domestic debt has risen sharply—from 23 percent of GDP in 1989 to 85 percent in 1995.

Political Risk. One important lesson is that the fiscal problems of the GCC states are essentially political in nature. Without exception, the governments suffer from structural deficits that are not inherently difficult to deal with, considering the capacity for increasing tax revenue. No GCC citizen pays income tax or sales tax, and as a rule, only foreign businesses pay any sort of corporate income tax. Similarly, curbing expenditures (and raising additional revenue) ought to be relatively simple, in principle, by increasing the price of public services and utilities to a level close to the cost of providing those benefits. The private sector can well afford increased charges and a modest level of taxation, and any short-term negative economic effects would be more than outweighed by the long-term benefits of a stabilized fiscal position. Yet, the government has not taken these easy measures; the preference has been to draw down foreign assets or accumulate debt.

This hesitancy to impose costs on their own populations may seem curious in light of the fact that the GCC rulers are all hereditary autocrats with the power to legislate by decree. The reality in the GCC states is that an implicit social contract exists under which the ruling family is granted broad authority in the political sphere but is expected to provide for the material well-being of the population. While oil prices were high, this task was almost effortless, and as benefits were conferred on the people, they developed a sense of entitlement. This feeling was encouraged by rulers who believed it strengthened their own legitimacy.

During the same time, GCC societies were undergoing rapid transformation. As a result, populations are now overwhelmingly young and are far better educated and better informed about the rest of the world than their parents were. Their expectations are higher also, and although they can understand the policy dilemmas created by low oil prices, many are inclined to believe that the government's budget problems stem equally from official corruption and mismanagement. In such an environment, rulers may fear that any attempt to force ordinary citizens to absorb the costs of adjustment would be likely to provoke demands for a greater voice in deciding the political and economic affairs of state.

▪ *Kuwait, the UAE, and Qatar.* These three GCC states are so small and so rich that they can probably carry on for some time without major reform, although doing so will likely entail an increasing drain on reserve assets. Of the three, Kuwait is perhaps the most interesting because of its experiment with a limited form of democracy. After five years of post-war existence, however, the assembly has largely confined itself to a watchdog role, auditing the government's performance and expenditures. There are no signs that the assembly might grow into an institution that, because of its popular legitimacy, could make difficult but necessary decisions on fiscal and economic reform. Nevertheless, political liberalization has given Kuwait a flexible and adaptable system that should enhance domestic stability.

▪ *Bahrain, Oman, and Saudi Arabia.* These three countries are in a different position from the small GCC states—Bahrain because its resource base is so small, Saudi Arabia and Oman because their populations are much larger than those of the other GCC states. Bahrain's regime is the only one in the GCC to face widespread popular opposition. The disadvantaged Shiite majority, as well as many of their Sunni compatriots, has focused on a call for political change in the form of a restoration of the suspended constitution and an elected assembly. The example of Kuwait's evolution toward democracy has undoubtedly led many Bahrainis to hope for something similar, and relative economic hardship has aggravated popular discontent. The government professes to see in the protests only economic dissatisfaction made worse by foreign interference. Political liberalization is effectively ruled out by Bahrain's dependence on Saudi Arabia, which is not likely to welcome liberalization. Financial and security assistance from its neighbors should ensure survival of Bahrain's government, but economic and fiscal reform will prove difficult in the strained political environment.

Oman differs from the other GCC states in a number of ways. Its economic and social development began only about 20 years ago, and that late start has affected its policies. Most importantly, the government has been determined not to create a lavish welfare state. Because of the country's large population and relatively modest resource base, Oman could not afford such largesse. Even Oman's limited system of social benefits will be difficult to sustain, however, without substantial modification.

Saudi Arabia's position is unique because of the size of its population and the complexity of its domestic political situation. The two car-bomb attacks on U.S. military personnel are evidence of some sort of violent opposition, but unlike Bahrain, no evidence of broad popular support for revolutionary change is visible in Saudi Arabia. Saudi society does contain disaffected groups, however, notably the Shiites of the oil-producing Eastern Province, many of whom feel they have suffered economic neglect and political discrimination. The ruling family has been the occasional target of criticism from both liberals and conservatives and is in the midst of a prolonged transfer of power from the ailing King Fahd to Crown Prince Abdullah.

Despite these difficult circumstances, one can argue that the Saudi government has done more than any of its neighbors to address the need for policy changes. The measures announced in its 1995 budget, which included increased charges for all public utilities and a nearly 100 percent increase in fuel prices, were accompanied by official warnings that difficult economic circumstances would inevitably require citizens to pay a greater share of the cost of government. Yet, it is a measure of this issue's sensitivity that King Fahd felt obliged at the time to assure his subjects that the measures were only temporary. In fact, they have been retained, although they have not been expanded. Particularly interesting is the Saudi population's reaction, or lack of reaction, to these measures. The notion that ordinary citizens should pay more for public services does not seem to have provoked much controversy.

In fact, GCC rulers may have overestimated the political sensitivity of fiscal reform. Certainly one of the greatest political risks facing the region is the possibility that the governments will postpone reform until too late out of fear of popular discontent.

Regional Security. Uncertainties about regional security impose an additional, but not uniform, constraint on the credit ratings. Even before Iraq's invasion of Kuwait in 1990, the GCC states appeared vulnerable to intimidation or aggression from their stronger neighbors in the Gulf. Since the Gulf War made that threat explicit, all six countries have had to reconsider their security arrangements. Joint security was part of the GCC's original *raison d'être*, and security remains at the heart of the group's agenda. Realistically, however, the GCC countries do not have the military strength to resist an attack on the scale of the 1990 Iraqi invasion. Because they must, therefore, rely on outside forces for military assistance, the GCC states' highest foreign policy priority has been to secure, in advance, reliable defense commitments from strategic partners.

Now more than ever, the GCC must rely on the West—especially the United States. Given the strategic importance of the Gulf region to the West, these arrangements are likely to prove durable, but they cannot provide absolute security. Moreover, close security ties with the West impose a number of financial and political costs on the GCC states. For example, all of them feel pressure, to a greater or lesser degree, to award military contracts to their Western defense partners, often in excess of their own legitimate requirements. In addition, the close and highly visible relationship between the GCC states and the West is politically awkward, at home and abroad. It tends to weaken the countries' ties to the rest of the Arab world, which may not be important in terms of military security but which does isolate the Gulf region from its own natural political and cultural spheres.

Of course, the security situation of each state is unique. Oman, for example, is scarcely in the Gulf at all. It is involved in regional strategic planning only by virtue of its membership in the GCC. Kuwait, in contrast, is almost surrounded by Iran, Iraq, and Saudi Arabia. The three other small Gulf states—Bahrain, the UAE, and Qatar—tend to be less concerned about Iraq than about Iran as the likeliest threat. Bahrain has accused Iran of fomenting unrest there. The UAE is involved in a territorial dispute with Iran, but it is careful to maintain correct relations because of, in part, Iran's importance as a trading partner. The UAE has also taken the lead in attempting to normalize relations with Iraq, as far as possible within the United Nations sanctions. The Saudi government also worries about Iran, with whom it has an uneasy relationship; Iran may be implicated in the Khobar bombing. Finally, Saudi Arabia has an ambivalent relationship with the rest of the GCC, which it far surpasses in size, population, and economic scale.

Demographics. Perhaps the most important factor shaping the future of the GCC countries is demographics. The World Bank estimates given in **Table 6** indicate that population growth rates in these six states are among the highest in the world. (Note that these data include resident foreigners, which explains why Kuwait's population shows a decline after 1990. Noncitizens make up about a third of the total, but their inclusion does not grossly distort the growth rate estimates.)

All these additional people will put enormous demand pressures on the GCC economies—above all, demand for public services and subsidized goods, which are underpriced. Electricity consumption, for example, is reported to have been increasing at 10 percent a year in Saudi Arabia, despite a fairly weak economy, largely because it is inexpensive. This growth requires investment in new generating capacity, but fiscal constraints have limited the capital budget's growth. Proposals to give the private sector a greater role in the provision of new infrastructure will work only if private investors are allowed to make a profit. Therefore, prices will have to rise or taxes will have to be imposed. In short, citizens will have to be asked to accept a decline in income.

These governments will find calling for more of people's income a hard task, but a much harder task

Table 6. Population in GCC Countries
(millions)

Country	1980	1985	1990	1995	Average Annual Increase
Saudi Arabia	9.37	12.38	14.87	17.88	4.4%
Kuwait	1.37	1.72	2.13	1.69	1.4
UAE	1.01	1.35	1.67	2.31	5.7
Oman	0.98	1.26	1.75	2.16	5.4
Bahrain	0.34	0.41	0.49	0.59	3.7
Qatar	0.23	0.36	0.49	0.59	6.5
Total	13.30	17.48	21.4	25.22	

still will be providing jobs for their young people. Because of the population growth rates, the GCC countries have among the youngest populations in the world. The labor force, therefore, will grow faster than the general population in these countries—probably for many years. Few GCC citizens are willing to take unskilled laboring positions, but large numbers of them lack the skills or require too much pay for most other jobs, which explains the staggeringly large number of foreign workers present in the Gulf. The small wealthy countries—Kuwait, the UAE, and Qatar—may be able to continue guaranteeing employment in the public sector for a long time, but jobs in the other three countries will have to come from the private sector.

Managing change on the scale needed to improve the fiscal, political, and employment situations in GCC states will not be easy. The most difficult aspect may be persuading a skeptical population that the changes must be made. For that reason, if the recent fall in oil prices can be used to make the case for new policies, that otherwise adverse trend might have a political silver lining.

Conclusion

Credit analysis for countries in most fairly well-defined regions of the world can be based on sensible generalizations about the economies, cultures, and histories of those regions. Such is decidedly not the case with the economies of Africa and the Middle East. About all one can say is that these economies tend to be resource based, reliant on exports of primary goods to the developed world, and characterized by a low level of integration with the global economy. And despite the fact that most governments in the region now accept the need for market-oriented policies, only a handful of countries have come far enough to become participants in bond markets.

Turkey, South Africa, and Israel offer potentially interesting prospects to global bond investors, and the six Gulf Cooperation Council states—Saudi Arabia, Kuwait, the UAE, Bahrain, Qatar, and Oman—present particularly intriguing challenges for credit analysts. Even in these cases, however, cloudy economic and political outlooks have, by and large, kept credit ceilings lower than would otherwise be the case.

… Africa and the Middle East

Question and Answer Session

David Larson

Question: Moody's A3 rating for Israel reflects the political and security risks arising from the future of the peace process. Does Moody's credit rating for Tunisia similarly incorporate the risk of the turmoil in Algeria spilling into Tunisia?

Larson: If Israel did not have the problem of regional insecurity and a difficult peace process, its rating would almost certainly be higher. In the case of Tunisia, however, we feel somewhat more comfortable that the risk of the problems in Algeria spilling over into Tunisia is small. We believe the moment of greatest risk for Tunisia has passed, and the situation for the Tunisians is stable.

Question: Do you expect South Africa to be added to any major fixed-income market index in the near future, and do you expect any corporate issuers from South Africa to tap Western bond markets?

Larson: I would not be surprised to see South Africa added to a fixed-income index. From a diversification point of view, South Africa is a unique credit because it is the only country in sub-Saharan Africa that is in the bond market. Also, it has the largest and most developed financial markets to be found in the Africa/Middle East region.

Some of the better-known corporate names in South Africa may be tempted by overseas issuance. At present, they may believe they would have to pay too rich a price for that move, but assuming that medium-term economic and policy developments in South Africa are favorable, the pricing situation might change.

Question: How will the Asian currency and credit crisis affect Moody's approach to credit analysis in Africa, or elsewhere?

Larson: We have all felt a bit humbled by the Asian experience. Moody's did downgrade Thailand back in 1996, but in retrospect, no one anticipated the virulence of the contagion that swept through Asia. None of us, for example, imagined that a credit rated as high as South Korea could be brought so low.

Consequently, we are increasing our focus on some key credit factors, including some identified by John Paulsen: liquidity, capital-account issues, short-term debt, and reserve cover for short-term debt.[2] Another aspect we are analyzing is whether changes in credit ratings should be more frequent than they have been. Fund managers have told us that such large adjustments as were made for Korea in such a short time are exceptionally awkward for them. We are aware that bond investors as a community are dominated by funds, especially in the emerging markets, so such considerations are important to us.

Perhaps the most important lesson is that we must all constantly remind ourselves that the next crisis will not be like the last one. We have to try to shake ourselves free from any sort of static framework of analysis. After the 1980s, for instance, the tendency was to look for trouble only from the Latin American countries, and that tendency clearly played a part in underrating the strength of the problems in Asia.

---
[2]See Mr. Paulsen's presentation, pp. 47–60.

©Association for Investment Management and Research

Corporate Credit Analysis: Latin America

Laura Feinland Katz
Director, Corporate Ratings
Standard & Poor's Corporation

> Analyzing corporate credit risk in Latin America has taken on increasing importance since issuers and investors have been rocked by repeated crises in emerging markets. The comprehensive framework recommended here for analyzing the creditworthiness of Latin American corporate borrowers incorporates sovereign risk assessment and evaluation of the borrower's competitive and financial positions.

In the very recent past, investors have been reminded anew and repeatedly of the risks faced by companies in emerging markets. With the devaluation of the Mexican peso in late 1994 and the so-called Asian contagion in late 1997/early 1998, both of which affected companies in emerging markets all over the world, credit risk in emerging markets has become an increasingly important topic. This presentation discusses several elements of the analytical process used by Standard & Poor's (S&P) to rate corporate credits in emerging markets and, more particularly, in Latin America; the presentation advocates a credit analysis framework that combines assessment of the impacts of sovereign risk on a company with traditional evaluation of the company's competitive and financial positions.

Impact of Sovereign Actions

The actions of a country affect the creditworthiness of the companies domiciled therein directly through intervention (the possibility of which is called "sovereign risk") and less directly through various policy decisions (the possibility of which is called "country risk").

Sovereign Risk. This term brings to mind most immediately the specter of the government (the sovereign) intervening directly in markets in a way that affects companies' abilities to meet offshore obligations. In this context, sovereign risk is also known as "transfer risk," which arises whenever a sovereign action calls into question an issuer's ability to access hard currency to service foreign debt. Such restrictive actions can take many forms—mandated moratoriums on external debt payments (or worse, nationalization of all private external debt), limits on the availability of foreign exchange, required repatriation of all offshore funds or export proceeds, dual or multiple exchange rates put in place by the sovereign, or simply general restrictions on capital movements. The potential effects of such intervention are so critical that the corporate credit ratings of the companies in a country and the country's foreign currency rating are typically constrained by the sovereign credit rating, a situation that creates the so-called sovereign ceiling.

Country Risk. Beyond the direct constraints on a company's ability to obtain foreign currency are more subtle constraints, the country risk factors. These factors are the economic, business, and social environments and conditions that affect the creditworthiness, or credit ratings, of the country's debt issues and the issues of those entities domiciled in the country. Country risk thus includes

- size, structure, growth, and volatility of the economy;
- exchange rates, inflation, interest rates, and associated policies;
- regulatory, tax, and legal issues;
- the country's infrastructure; and
- labor market conditions in the country.

The same conditions that put a country's sovereign credit under stress also put the credit of the companies domiciled in the country under stress. This connection is as true for recent events in Indonesia as it was for Latin America in the 1980s and Mexico in the mid-1990s.

Economic structure. A sovereign's decisions and policies most directly affect growth trends and cyclicality in the country's economy. Is the sovereign pursuing policies that will likely produce strong booms and busts? If so, the performance of any company in that country, particularly one in a cyclical industry, will be more cyclical than would otherwise be the case.

Exchange rate policy. The sovereign's stance on exchange rate management is crucial; exchange rate volatility directly affects (1) the profitability of companies that have costs and revenues in different currencies and (2) the debt-servicing requirements of the companies.

Regulatory and tax issues. Opportunities for country risk are present in regulatory issues and tax issues, because changes frequently amount to "changing the rules of the game." Sovereigns, particularly in times of stress, will do what they need to do to protect their interests, which often involves changing the regulatory environment in which companies operate and/or tax laws with which companies must comply.

Legal issues. Changes in laws and enforcement also affect how companies operate. Particularly important to credit analysis are creditors' rights, which differ substantially from country to country, and the extent to which contracts are binding and enforceable. The ability to enforce bondholder rights in major Latin American countries (Colombia, Mexico, Brazil, Argentina) may be weak or untested. The notable exception among the major countries is Chile; the Chilean legal system offers the strongest protections in the region. Argentina's trust law also affords some protections to creditors who have structured transactions to take advantage of that law.

Where the legal code has not been updated to provide for modern bankruptcy proceedings, predicting what will happen in a bankruptcy or other type of reorganization is difficult. Mexico exemplifies those countries where investors and others have a hard time predicting what will happen if creditors start legal actions. For that reason, the reorganizations in Mexico are not usually through formal proceedings, such as bankruptcy. Rather, the creditors and the issuer go through an informal process.

These aspects may vary in magnitude and subtlety, but one clear implication is the absolute necessity of incorporating the regional complexities facing a company into any basic credit analysis framework. Effective corporate credit analysis in emerging markets, especially those in Latin America, will proceed from an understanding of individual countries and regional complexities to a basic framework that is similar to that for a company in a developed market, a framework that focuses on the competitive and financial positions of the borrower.

Competitive Position

A key component of credit analysis is analyzing the company's competitive position—within the country where it resides and globally. Although the company's business environment is inextricably linked to the sovereign's policies and actions, certain characteristics of the specific environment, as well as characteristics of the company's ownership and management, are important determinants of the company's competitiveness. In addition to standard credit analysis factors, such as market share or cost competitiveness, the analysis of Latin American companies should consider the impact of exchange rate volatility, regulatory risk, the labor environment, infrastructure, trade barriers, and local industry structure.

Operating Efficiency and Exchange Rates. The operating efficiency of a company is critical to its competitive position, especially in terms of exchange rate impact. For example, prior to the devaluation of the peso in late 1994, some mining and metal companies in Mexico were struggling to be competitive. Because the peso had been appreciating before the devaluation, these Mexican companies' costs were high compared with those of global competitors. Of course, that situation reversed completely with the devaluation of the peso in December 1994. Analysts looking at these companies through 1995 would have seen that their cost positions looked very favorable, particularly those companies that had largely local-currency cost bases, even though some companies may have had difficulties attracting financing. In 1995, these companies were "world-class" competitors. Inflation eventually caught up with the devaluation level of the peso, however, and to some extent, the tables turned. Measures of operating efficiency deteriorated as the peso appreciated in relative terms.

The key lesson is the need, particularly in a cyclical industry and particularly in an emerging economy, to look at many years of historical data to understand how a company has been affected by relative currency valuations at different points in the cycle.

Regulatory Risk. Changes in government regulations can drastically affect how a company operates. A recent example is MCI Telecommunications' investment in long-distance phone service in Mexico. MCI entered that market with optimistic expectations, particularly about the price it would need to pay Telefonos de México for access to the local lines. According to MCI's announcements in February 1998, that cost shifted so substantially that it is no longer consistent with earlier expectations. In fact, MCI has announced major reductions in its investment plan.

Regulatory risk is particularly important for utilities and their pricing policies. In Argentina, for example, the two major telephone companies have written approval from all the regulatory bodies to link their pricing to the U.S. dollar and, in fact, to compensate for U.S. dollar inflation. Although a devaluation in Argentina is not expected (because the currency is linked one-to-one with the U.S. dollar), that pricing structure would, in theory, shelter the companies from any devaluation. If Argentina had a currency devaluation, however, and returned to a hyperinflationary scenario, the country would be unlikely to allow basic providers of services to increase prices in line with the devaluation. Such a move would not be politically palatable. So, regulatory risk should be kept in mind in any analysis of the creditworthiness of a company operating in Argentina. Indeed, this regulatory risk is keeping Argentine telephone companies from being rated even higher above the sovereign credit than is already the case. S&P has rated these companies BBB– (against the sovereign's BB), but the companies actually have strong BBB+ or even A credit levels. The potential regulatory pressure with respect to pricing constrains the rating. Specifically, that constraint is translated into the rating by looking at reasonable expectations of cash flows in the future and analyzing the sensitivity of those cash flows to a severe devaluation. Such a scenario analysis turns what might otherwise be an A-rated company into a BBB– company.

Labor Environment. A country's labor environment must also be taken into consideration when conducting company credit analyses. Strikes are announced periodically in the Brazilian port cities, for instance, and trucking strikes are common in Colombia.

Infrastructure. A country's physical infrastructure may also limit a company's ability to conduct business. For instance, poor roads or mismanaged railroads make shipping goods difficult for many companies.

Trade Barriers. Trade barriers are particularly critical for analyzing companies in emerging markets. Companies may be competitive in their existing environments, but if trade barriers are phased out as part of some regional or global agreement, the companies' global competitiveness may be put to the test.

Many countries have recently made progress in opening their economies to competition. The Mercosur Trade Agreement has enhanced trade flows among Brazil, Argentina, Uruguay, and Paraguay, and some countries in the northern part of South America are considering joining Mercosur to enlarge that trade conference. Mexico has entered the North American Free Trade Agreement, so barriers have come down. But analysts still need to pay attention to countries where trade barriers of some type still exist. Also, certain industries that are currently protected in trade pacts, such as the auto industry in Mercosur, may eventually face free competition.

Local Industry Structure. The structure of local industries can be either a positive or a negative for a company. One must understand what the industry looks like globally for those companies competing globally, regionally for companies competing regionally, and locally for all companies.

Particularly important is that analysts not expect industries to behave in other parts of the world as they do in the United States. The cement industry, for example, is a very fragmented industry in the United States; it is a tough competitive environment for most producers. The cement industry in Mexico is drastically different: Two producers control the vast majority of the market, which makes the industry environment much more stable. The Mexican cement industry is also retail-brand conscious; the companies have made a point of using brand management successfully, which makes their competitive positions much stronger than is usual in many more-developed economies around the world. On the other hand, Mexico has a volatile macroeconomic environment. The outlook for housing construction, which is a result of government policy to expand the housing supply in Mexico, is bolstering long-term demand for cement. When recessionary conditions occur, however, as they did in late 1994, 1995, and 1996, local cement demand drops more than it might elsewhere in the world and competition is tough. The analyst must weigh such potentially offsetting factors in any judgment about creditworthiness.

Another example of the importance of local industry structure is the cellular phone industry. The outlook for the industry appears to be favorable in many Latin American countries, where access to phone lines is a problem. In some countries, people either have to wait six months to a year to get a phone or they have to pay someone to get it sooner, so phone access is either time consuming or expensive. Therefore, a demand exists for rapid phone service, which is precisely what cellular technology can do. In Latin America, however, the industry quickly hits an income barrier. Per capita incomes in Latin America are much lower than in the United States, for example. Thus, analysts must weigh local demand against local demographics and other features when analyzing the potential for any industry.

Structure and Ownership. Another important determinant of competitive position is a company's ownership and management structure, particularly as that structure affects its business strategy. These considerations, although important anywhere, are absolutely critical in analyzing companies in emerging markets. In Latin America, as in many parts of Asia, many of the major companies are controlled by family conglomerates. This structure can add "umbrella" support for all companies of the group, but analysts need to keep in mind that a weak member of the group can adversely affect other group members, even those that have apparently strong business positions and solid financial structures. The *chaebols* in South Korea are such an example.

In Mexico, for instance, a steel company that was performing relatively well (Grupo Simec) was affected by the poor performance of a sister company in the group (Grupo Situr) that focused on the tourism and real estate industry. Situr's problems brought down the entire group (Grupo Sidek); all the companies ended up restructuring their debt.

Understanding a group's financial policies and track record is especially important. Some groups have policies to keep each company separate and not commingle any of the finances. Some groups do not. Analysts may be taking a certain amount of comfort from the track record of a high-performing company and may project good performance in the future, but the actual results may well depend on the track record of weak links of the group.

Financial Position

As important and complex as issues of competitive position are, issues of financial position—risk management, accounting, profitability, capital structure, cash flow, and flexibility—are critical for companies domiciled in Latin America. Analysts must try to understand how a company's management, through financial policies, is compensating for the risks of its business environment. For example, companies in volatile business environments should have relatively conservative financial policies and structures to compensate for that volatility.

Risk Management. Foreign exchange hedging and matching are the important tools of risk management. Hedges that are standard for currencies elsewhere are typically not available in Latin America, are very expensive, or are only short term in nature. One- or two-year hedges can sometimes be purchased, but an exposure involving a medium-term horizon cannot be hedged. This condition explains why many Latin American companies are not hedging foreign exchange risk. Analysts should look to see that companies are at least trying to match their debt structures, in terms of currency and tenor, to their cash flows.

A company's arbitrage policies also must be understood. Many companies in Brazil are currently taking advantage of arbitrage opportunities. In particular, exporters who get dollar-based credit at a reasonable cost are being tempted to invest back in Brazil, either in the local currency (reais), which will earn current Brazilian interest rates of 35 percent or so, or in a Brazilian government dollar instrument that pays in reais but is linked to the U.S. dollar, which will earn in the 14–15 percent range. Because these exporters could be borrowing at 8–10 percent, either investment is tempting. Of course, the opportunities entail either currency risk or Brazilian government risk, which could have adverse future consequences. Analysts need to understand what is driving the risk-management policies of companies and how those policies should affect analysis of companies' financial policies in general.

Accounting and Disclosure Issues. Because of obvious differences in accounting systems, most companies in Latin America (and in emerging market countries in general) provide disclosure that is neither as timely nor as complete as the disclosure provided by companies in the United States. Thus, analysts need to try to draw out this information when meeting with company personnel. If they do not have that access, they at least need to understand key potential accounting differences.

■ *Consolidation.* Often, consolidated reporting is not required in the home country, so companies may or may not choose to provide it.

■ *Segment disclosure.* Segment disclosure, which is often critical for understanding how the different parts of a company are performing, is not usually available.

■ *Inflation accounting.* Inflation accounting is a fact of life in most Latin American countries. Many countries have recently reduced their inflation levels: Argentina's recent inflation rate has been 1–2 percent, and Brazil has its inflation rate down to single digits. In these countries, however (and even in countries that have low inflation rates historically), analysts must understand the impact that inflation accounting has had over the years, particularly on asset values.

■ *Interest expense disclosure.* In Latin American countries, interest expense disclosure, which is taken for granted in the United States, is often not what analysts expect. For example, Brazilian statements often provide disclosure only of "net financial expense," which can include interest income, interest expense, noncash monetary correction, and foreign exchange transaction gains and losses. This practice makes determining coverage of fixed charges difficult.

Profitability. A focus on recurring operating earnings allows the analyst to make judgments about a company's real, sustained profitability. Analysts also need to understand what foreign exchange rate distortions are doing to a company's relative profitability. Is there a currency mismatch in the revenues versus costs, and how might that mismatch change the profit picture in the future?

Pricing flexibility will be particularly important for producers of basic goods in the event of a return to inflation linked with devaluation. Analysts need to consider the effect that inflation and devaluation would have on a company's margins, assuming the company cannot fully pass along the increases in its cost base because of formal or informal government regulation of pricing behavior.

The risk from dependence on imports is currently exemplified in Indonesia. Companies that need to import are facing a drastic increase in the cost of those imports in local-currency terms. Exporters that rely on imported components, and investors in those exporters, must recognize two potential risks to these exporters' ongoing profitability: first, that the imported components will be difficult to obtain because the importing companies cannot access credit at a reasonable cost and, second, that the imported components will be much more expensive than originally anticipated.

Capital Structure. Analyzing the capital structure of a company in a country with a history of hyperinflation, such as Brazil or Argentina, is particularly challenging, even if the inflationary environment no longer exists.

Asset valuation. Typically, the accounting systems dealt with past inflation by allowing companies to write up asset values in line with inflation every year. The increases in asset values were, in turn, offset by increases in equity. This procedure was preferable to not correcting for inflation; otherwise, hyperinflation would have destroyed the value of the assets. The problem is, and it is particularly acute in the case of capital-intensive companies, that the asset values and equity positions that appear today on these companies' balance sheets may or may not bear any relationship to actual market-determined levels. Thus, trying to judge a company's leverage based on balance-sheet-based ratios can be misleading, so analysts need to focus that much more on cash flow indicators.

Debt structure. In addition to trying to make sense of a company's asset values, analysts need to understand the company's debt structure. The maturity of debt is especially critical. During the Tequila Crisis, many Mexican companies depended heavily on short-term Euro commercial paper issues, which they had been accustomed to rolling over without any difficulties. In December 1994, that source of credit was eliminated virtually overnight; it was either prohibitively expensive or was simply not available. Those companies that had been relying on short-term rollovers of this type suddenly became quite capital constrained. The best companies were able to turn to their bank lenders, either foreign or in Mexico, but Mexican banks' available credit lines were drastically reduced because the banking system was in a credit crunch. The weak companies faced great difficulties. So, analysts must make a distinction between short- and long-term maturities; excessive reliance on short-term debt can, in a crisis, translate into seriously diminished access to credit.

Currency. The currency mismatch that arises from having cash flow in one currency and debt in another is an important aspect of creditworthiness. In Mexico before December 1994, some companies that were primarily local-currency generators had borrowed in dollars, either because it seemed like a relatively cheap source of financing or because it was the only source of long-term financing. With the devaluation of the peso, these companies' earning power was reduced by half in relation to their debts virtually overnight, although inflation allowed them to earn back the difference—with a substantial time lag. Again, the possibility of such a mismatch means that ratios, particularly any kind of balance-sheet-based leverage ratios, must be looked at with a skeptical eye. A better approach than examining ratios is scenario analysis based on critical drivers. If a company is a local-currency generator with a dollar debt structure, for instance, the analyst should not focus on today's ratios but should look at reasonable devaluation scenarios to analyze how drastically a devaluation would change the type of credit protection the company has.

Cash Flow Analysis. Because of all the capital structure issues, cash flow analysis is much more useful than balance sheet analysis in judging the creditworthiness of Latin American companies. S&P uses such measures as cash flow relative to debt outstanding, cash flow relative to capital expenditures, and operating free cash flow relative to debt-service requirements.

The fact that many Latin American companies are part of large corporate groups means that analysts must always be alert to the potential cash drains caused when a company is required to forward cash to the controlling group. Examples abound of holding companies in Mexico virtually mandating that group companies take on substantial amounts of debt, the only purpose of which is to provide cash dividends to the parent. Thus, the context for the demands on cash flow, particularly the dividend policy of the parent, is certainly important.

Legal dividend minimums create further complexity for cash flow analysis. For example, in Chile and Brazil, companies must pay out, respectively, 30 percent and 25 percent of net profits. The positive aspect of such a policy is that everyone in the marketplace understands that companies' dividends will vary with profits; investors in these countries do not expect to see a steadily rising dividend per share. The policy is a constraint, however, in that it reduces the companies flexibility to use the cash for other purposes.

Financial Flexibility. Financial flexibility is one of the key constraints for companies in emerging markets, if for no other reason than because of the myriad risks that reside in such markets. Accordingly, assessing financial flexibility should emphasize the borrowing company's potential responses to events that endanger the creditor's position. What will be the company's access to local and/or international credit, and what will be the company's options under stress?

Access to local/international credit. In the wake of the Asian crisis of late 1997, even the best companies in Latin America either were not able to issue bonds at all or found the cost of doing so prohibitive—all because the crisis in Asia increased perceptions of risk in emerging markets in general. And the 1997 situation is not a one-time event. For the first several months in early 1995, no Latin American company was able to go to the bond markets; again, investors were not buying the paper or were demanding too high a price.

The lesson is that access to capital markets may not have anything to do with the company or even its country; investors' general expectations can affect a company's ability to access capital. So, analysts need to understand that companies face windows of access to the capital markets that continually close and open. And they need to understand the particular factors that may help free a company from these sorts of constraints—in particular, its local status. The best companies in the markets typically have access to bank credit. That is, if any bank credit is available locally, it tends to go to the best companies. The best companies also tend to continue to receive access to capital from the international banks, assuming that those banks are lending in the country at all.

The depth of the local capital market is critical. Unfortunately, in Latin America, most local capital markets are not deep, which is why the companies are so dependent on foreign capital. Chile is one of the exceptions; it has a well-developed capital market that enjoys important participation from the local pension funds. The existence of a well-developed local capital market is a major reason why companies in Chile were among the least affected by the otherwise broad Latin American crisis in 1995. The banks in Chile were in better shape than the banks in other Latin American countries at the time, which certainly helped local companies, but Chile also had a reasonably deep and liquid local bond market.

The Argentine private pension fund system has grown substantially; assets under management are now estimated to be US$10 billion, or 3 percent of GDP, compared with 40 percent of GDP for the much older Chilean system. Mexico launched a private pension system in mid-1997, and the estimate is that 80 percent of eligible employees have affiliated with the private pension funds, known by their Spanish acronym, Afores.

When looking at companies in the United States, analysts take committed bank lines for granted as a sign of credit access and source of liquidity. In Latin America during the past two decades, however, companies simply have not been able to obtain committed credit lines because banks rarely extended such lines. This lack of committed credit lines has affected all companies in Latin America. Change may be occurring, however, albeit slowly; CEMEX, a Mexican cement company, was recently able to arrange a committed credit line with a group of international banks. Some companies have also been able to participate in programs providing U.S. commercial paper backed by letters of credit. Such programs serve the same function as committed credit lines because the bank is backing the paper for at least a year. Commercial paper programs helped many companies in Mexico in 1995. The general rule for Latin American companies is still, however, that they do not get committed credit lines. In the absence of such commitments, banks (and, consequently, investors) tend to flee when a country has serious problems, and their absence is another constraint on the companies' financial flexibility.

Access to export credit, if it exists, can and does serve to partially offset the constraints on financial flexibility. Fortunately, most Latin American governments have established formal procedures for extending credit to exporters. Brazil is one example. Exporting companies get far better borrowing terms than almost any other company because of the government's well-developed policy for providing trade financing to the companies. The problem is that nonexporting companies are then at even more of a relative disadvantage in the economy.

Regional issues can also constrain a company's financial flexibility. The Tequila Crisis affected companies in Brazil, Chile, Colombia, and Argentina in 1995, even though the original problem was in Mexico. The lesson is that, although a company may be based in a country that seems to be performing well, the company may be exposed to shifts of international investor confidence.

Options under stress. The situations that put stress on a company's financial flexibility are often an extension of a sovereign's stress. Thus, analysts need to determine what the company's reasonable options will be in such stressful circumstances. Does the company have the opportunity to sell assets or entire businesses? These options are a source of flexibility, but the time when asset sales will be the most difficult and values the lowest is precisely when a country is in crisis. In general, parent commitment and/or geographical diversity are more meaningful measures of a company's ability to withstand sovereign stress; in fact, the presence of these factors can cause a corporate credit to trade above the corresponding sovereign credit—that is, to "trade through the sovereign ceiling."

Parent commitment can be especially powerful if the parent is an offshore multinational. An example is Coca Cola's operation in Mexico, which is called Coca-Cola FEMSA. This company has a higher foreign currency credit rating than Mexico itself. The logic is that during a period that seems to be "temporarily" difficult, in terms of the behavior of the sovereign and the economic conditions in the country, Coca-Cola could step in to support the subsidiary because the parent takes the long-term view that Mexico is a strategic place to do business. Depending on the strategic value of the subsidiary to the parent, then, and the track record of the parent, parent commitment can be an important means of sheltering a company through a crisis.

Geographical diversity, in the form of offshore assets or the ability to go outside the country and generate enough cash flow to support debt payment even if the company is prohibited from access to dollars in its home country, greatly enhances a company's financial flexibility. In many cases, even exporters are subject to sovereign constraints; when the sovereign is rationing dollars, it will often require exporters to repatriate export proceeds (e.g., deposit the proceeds, typically with a central bank, and reapply to get the amounts necessary for debt servicing, imports, or paying dividends). Thus, if a company has offshore operations that are relatively out of reach of the sovereign, offshore assets can be an important source of flexibility.

When, in the wake of the Tequila Crisis, CEMEX was facing difficult conditions in its home country of Mexico, it was able to weather the storm largely because of cash flows from its offshore operations—Spain in particular and Venezuela to a lesser extent. S&P has raised Panamco's ratings above that of its sovereign, Mexico, for similar reasons. Panamco is a Mexican-based bottler with operations divided equally among Mexico, Brazil, Colombia, and more recently, Central America and Venezuela. Panamco should thus have enough cash flow from more stable countries to service its dollar debts. The lesson is that a company that has substantial actual operations in a diverse array of countries, beyond even its export capabilities, has an additional important source of financial flexibility.

Conclusion

When conducting corporate credit analysis of companies in emerging markets, analysts must take local and regional factors and constraints into consideration. The companies of Latin America are no exception. Certain key factors—sovereign risk, competitive position, and financial position—should permeate every aspect of analysts' judgments about the creditworthiness of Latin American corporate borrowers.

Question and Answer Session
Laura Feinland Katz

Question: In the context of cheap exports into world markets, which Latin American industries are most affected by the Asian crisis?

Feinland Katz: This issue has become important from the perspective of major exporters and of companies being faced with competition from cheaper imports. Many Latin American exporters, which generally have been quite cost competitive, are now in a more difficult competitive environment from a global perspective. So, we are carefully reviewing, for example, the steel companies in the major steel-exporting countries—Mexico, Brazil, and Argentina. We are also closely studying the commodities exporters in Chile (the pulp companies and the copper exporters) in terms of where they can send their exports and the additional pricing constraints that have affected those commodities.

Question: Are certain natural resources more valuable than others in determining sovereign credit quality in Latin America?

Feinland Katz: The natural resource base is one of many factors in any sovereign rating. The type of resource matters less than its availability and, most important, how countries have used that resource to their advantage. For example, we have a rating of A– on Chile, which is very dependent on imported petroleum but rich in copper. We have only a B+ rating on Venezuela, although it has a roughly 60 billion barrel reserve base of oil. Petroleum reserves are critical, but Venezuela has not managed those reserves productively in terms of sheltering its economy from volatility or in terms of having a consistent macroeconomic policy. We factor into the rating the inconsistency in its management of that oil wealth. Our current rating reflects the fact that the government's budget revenue projections may fall short because Venezuela is highly dependent on oil revenues and oil price volatility is high.

Question: How will the reduction in foreign exchange reserves affect Chilean companies?

Feinland Katz: Chile is the Latin American country whose trade flows have been most affected by the crisis in Asia. Because of its location on the Pacific Rim, much of its trade has been destined for Asia. We have factored into the Chilean rating (currently at A–) its exposure to commodity risk and to the impact that current situations may have on the country in general and its foreign exchange reserve position in particular. Dependence on commodity exports has always constrained the Chilean rating. Investors could reasonably have looked at the Chilean credit ratios six months ago and have thought, "Why is this only an A– rating?" The answer is commodity export risk.

As for specific companies, although we believe they are helped by the reasonably solid macroenvironment implied by the sovereign rating, we have done a company-by-company analysis of how companies, particularly major exporters, are being affected by the situation in Asia. We look at whether the companies have been able to adjust by shipping their products elsewhere and whether they have been able to adjust to a lower-commodity-pricing environment. Most of the Chilean companies we rate in the natural resource sector have competitive cost positions. They are the companies that in low-pricing environments—such as for copper or pulp currently—are still profitable when many other global competitors are not.

Question: Why do some corporate debt issues trade through the sovereign ceiling even in the absence of parent protection or geographical diversity?

Feinland Katz: Some very strong corporate issuers do trade through the sovereign ceiling, presumably because the market believes they are solid enough to withstand a sovereign default. S&P has announced a "dollarization" criterion that provides for specific cases where we believe transfer risk (the ability to access U.S. dollars) is not constrained by the sovereign rating—that is, cases where corporate ratings and bond spreads should reflect less risk than the sovereign dollar bond rating.

In Argentina, for example, we think that the foreign currency rating of the sovereign, which is BB, does not reflect the true risk that companies face in terms of being able to access dollars. We think the amount of dollars flowing through the economy together with other factors, including the use of dollars in contracts and as a substantial part of banking system deposits, make it much less likely that the sovereign, even in a time of stress, would restrict the access of a company in that economy to U.S. dollars. So, we have raised some companies' ratings, based on their own creditworthiness, up to two notches above the sovereign.

A few companies in Argentina, for instance, have a BBB– rating on their dollar issues versus the sovereign rating of BB. We are not saying that stress in Argentina at that BBB– level is impossible. In fact, we still believe a BB type default risk of the sovereign is an implicit constraint for Argentine corporate credits. Certainly, the BB level implies that if the sovereign defaults, the economy will experience all kinds of dislocations—possibly a devaluation, a return to inflation, and many other challenges for companies. We put a company's rating above the sovereign BB rating if we make sure that the company has protections from such economic dislocations through its export operations, a conservative debt structure, and/or its ability to generate solid cash flows to meet its debt obligations. In other words, we raise the rating if we think the company will have the ability to generate enough local currency to access needed dollars.

Question: In light of the International Monetary Fund's (IMF's) recent involvement in Asia and the implication that a lender of last resort now exists that will bail out sovereigns when they get into default situations, is the sovereign risk premium changing?

Feinland Katz: Some countries are geopolitically important enough that we may expect to see rescue packages, but in any given case, we should count on neither a rescue package nor the desired result of that package occurring. The results of a rescue package are never guaranteed. The IMF makes those kinds of judgments on a case-by-case basis, and so should investors. Thus, any systematic change in the sovereign risk premium is unlikely.

The same conclusion applies for other types of assistance. Our rating of Mexico and our current view of the Mexican economy factor in Mexico's special relationship with the United States. The supportive action that the United States took in the spring of 1995 was critical for strengthening the Mexican economy and for restoring investor confidence in countries that the United States considers vitally important. Should investors count on that type of U.S. support in another crisis? Perhaps, but the answer depends a great deal on the level of congressional support.

Asian Lessons and Outlook

John Paulsen
Vice President
J.P. Morgan and Company

> The recent Asian crisis was triggered by changes in key fundamental economic factors in the region. Those changes provide insights for analyzing both sovereign and corporate credits in emerging markets. Asia's long-term prospects are still positive, but substantial differences exist among countries with respect to the pace of recovery and subsequent development.

The recent turmoil in the Asian financial markets—the so-called Asian flu or Asian contagion—has led analysts and investors to rethink many of their assumptions with respect to analyzing sovereign and corporate credits, not only in Asia but in all emerging markets. This presentation explores possible causes of the Asian crisis, sets forth some lessons to be learned from the crisis, and provides a regional and country-by-country outlook for selected Asian economies.

The Triggers

No crisis of such magnitude and far-reaching consequences as the Asian experience has simple causes. The roots of the crisis lie in six key economic factors—savings, investment financing, internal leverage, short-term external debt, current-account deficits, and real exchange rates.

Savings. During the past five years or so, the sovereign debt of Asian countries has been of relatively high quality. All the countries except the Philippines have been well into the investment-grade rating category and, until only recently, have experienced steady credit upgrades. That positive credit picture was the result of a track record of spectacular growth and development, which, in turn, was driven by one of the key characteristics of the region, one that remains in place even after the latest crisis: high domestic savings. As shown in **Figure 1**, the savings rate in Asia has been 25 percent of GDP or more since 1980 and, since 1990, has been rising. Current Asian savings rates are higher than the savings rates in Latin America or Eastern Europe by at least 10–15 percent of GDP.

Asia's savings rates remain a virtue and will be a key ingredient in the next few years in helping the region recover from the current crisis. One of the lessons to be learned from past Latin crises is that savings rates need to rise to reduce reliance on foreign debt capital.

Investment Financing. Where the Asian countries made mistakes was in how they invested this huge stock of savings. The quantity of investment was not the problem; the level of investment for most of the countries increased greatly in the 1990s, with aggressive investment in a variety of areas—both infrastructure and manufacturing. The manufacturing bases of some of the Asian economies developed rapidly, and the countries made progress in terms of moving the broad base of the economy up the development scale, out of high-labor-content exports and into more value-added exports.

Much of the progress was achieved by relatively inefficient investment, however, in part because of the quality of the financial sector. A large part of this investment activity was financed by domestic lending. The financial systems in many of these countries were fairly immature, however; while the broad economies, particularly the tradable goods and export sectors, were modernizing, the financial sectors remained relatively primitive—from the standpoint of sophistication of products and openness to foreign capital influence. For example, South Korea's development policy, which was closely modeled on Japan's, was designed so that a government-controlled financial system could take high levels of Korean savings and divert them to Korean industry at the lowest possible cost over time. This policy was not particularly attractive to

©Association for Investment Management and Research

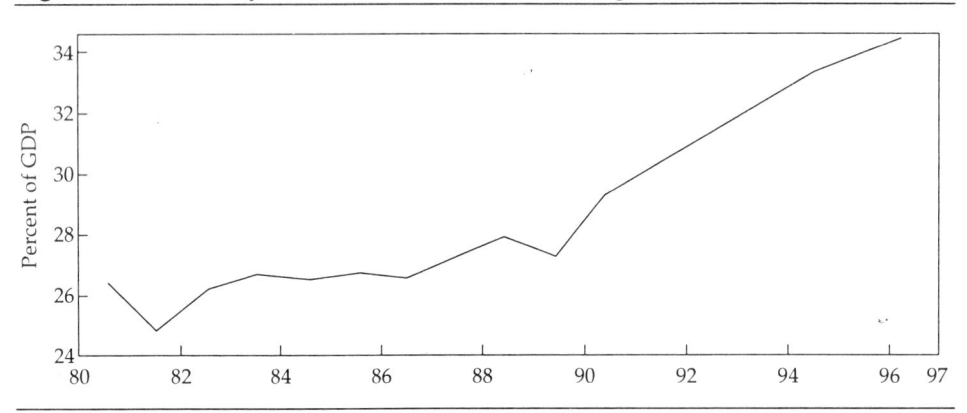

Figure 1. Fixed Capital Formation as a Percentage of GDP, 1980–97

Korean savers, but they had no choice in the matter. The net result was that the capital provided to Korean industry was mostly in the form of debt. This approach worked well for several decades to finance the growth of, from a product point of view, some world-class competitive corporations, but it left them highly leveraged and vulnerable to a slowdown in growth.

Internal Leverage. One of the leading indicators of this kind of internal financing in a country is loan growth over time, which measures the level of credit expansion by the banking sector to private industry. By this indicator, internal leverage is high in most Asian economies, as shown in **Figure 2**. Figure 2 is not measuring external indebtedness or the level of government debt within the country. Rather, it indicates private-sector indebtedness—loans provided by banks in the local country to private-sector borrowers in that country. The y-axis shows loan growth compared with GDP growth; the 100 percent level indicates that loan growth equals nominal GDP growth, which would be a relatively realistic assumption. An emerging market might well expect to experience a slightly higher level of such growth, but Figure 2 clearly shows that in a number of cases, levels of loan growth are well in excess of 150 percent. The x-axis shows the level of overall indebtedness of the private sector as a percentage of GDP, which is the most direct measure of how much internal leverage is in the economy.

The danger zone in Figure 2 is the upper right-hand corner—the area of high relative loan growth on top of an already heavily indebted economy. This danger zone contains five of the Asian countries that have experienced problems. This private-sector loan growth has had different objectives in different countries—financing property development and other infrastructure projects in Thailand and

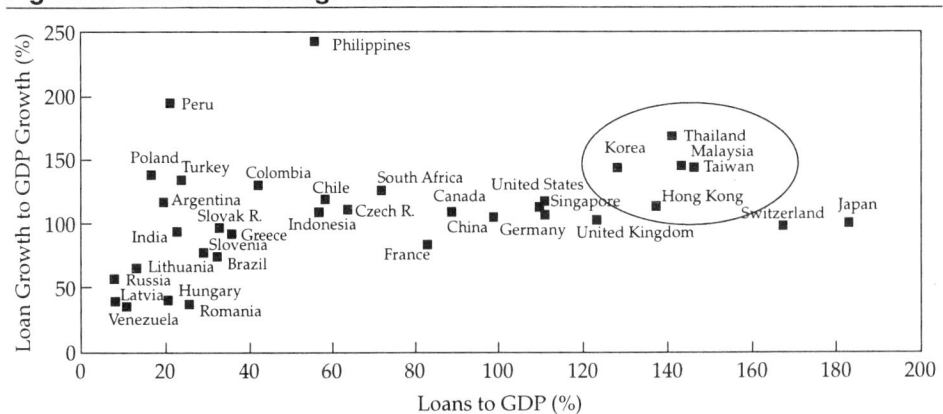

Figure 2. Internal Leverage: Loan Growth/GDP Growth versus Loans/GDP

Notes: Loan growth/GDP growth measured since year-end 1990; loans/GDP measured as of year-end 1996. The following East European countries' loan growth ratios were calculated using the GDP figures for different years: Czech Republic (1993), Latvia (1993), Lithuania (1994), Poland (1991), Romania (1991), Russia (1993), Slovak Republic (1993), and Slovenia (1991).

Sources: Based on data from J.P. Morgan and the International Monetary Fund Financial Statistics Database.

Malaysia and lending with equity shares as collateral in Malaysia. The problem in the case of Korea was that the private-sector debt was financing overinvestment in manufacturing.

Many analysts of sovereign debt clearly missed the signals being provided by these trends in internal leverage in the Asian economies, probably because internal leverage has not been a substantial factor in past analyses of a country's ability to service its external debt obligations. In an environment of open capital flows, however, internal leverage does matter. It creates conditions, particularly when GDP growth slows down, of extreme financial weakness in many of the interbank counterparties in the countries.

Such weak financial systems have inevitable consequences for the credit markets. **Table 1** reports some of the impact on the Asian developing countries and on Japan. The "Loans/GDP" column is the same relationship shown on the x-axis in Figure 2. (There are slight differences between the figure and the table because Figure 2 uses averages over seven years whereas Table 1 gives the estimate for 1998.) The data estimated for 1998 for the average level of nonperforming loans of the banks in each country reveal that the major problem countries in the Asian developing world are Korea, Thailand, Malaysia, and Indonesia. Depending on what happens to exchange rates in the near term, the number for Indonesia is probably substantially understated.

The nonperforming loans have a direct impact on sovereign creditworthiness because, by and large, the governments are going to have to bail out these banking systems. The governments will have to prop up the weak banks to provide a financial system that will be capable of financing recovery from the current recession. The last column in Table 1 gives estimates of the recapitalization costs to the governments of restructuring these nonperforming loans into some type of loan workouts. The worst case, excluding Japan, is Korea with a forecasted recapitalization cost of about US$155 billion. Based on estimated GDP for 1998, the recapitalization cost is equivalent to about 45 percent of Korean GDP.

Short-Term External Debt. Another problem that led to the Asian market crisis, particularly in November and December of 1997, is that the countries involved relied heavily on short-term external debt, much of which was interbank placements to the financial institutions in those countries. As shown in Panel A of **Figure 3**, leading up to the crisis, short-term debt was 40–50 percent of total external debt in most of the worst-affected countries. The important question for the future is whether cash resources will be available to meet repayments if that short-term debt cannot be rolled over. Panel B of Figure 3 explains why not all of these countries were equally affected by their reliance on short-term external debt. Malaysia, which was probably affected least during the first part of the Asian crisis, had foreign currency reserves equal to nearly twice its short-term debt. Korea, which has the highest proportion of short-term debt and has had the most severe problems, had almost no reserve coverage, less than 20 percent, of its short-term debt. Korea's reserve coverage had been at this low level for several years; it was a problem before confidence collapsed.

Current-Account Deficits. A country's current-account deficit is the level of investment that has not been financed by domestic savings. The size and (more importantly) financing of the countries' current-account deficits were also contributing factors to the Asian crisis. **Figure 4** shows the current-account deficits as a percentage of GDP and the extent to which those deficits were financed by debt inflows. Although Asian savings rates were and are high,

Table 1. Asian Banking Systems: Potential Costs of Bad Loans

Country	Loans/GDP	1998 Estimated Nonperforming Loans	Recapitalization Cost (US$ billions)
Hong Kong	175%	8%	NA
India	40	10	7
Indonesia	75	30	22
Korea	165	30	155
Malaysia	165	20	27
Philippines	60	12	0
Singapore	115	10	NA
Thailand	155	30	52
Average or total	119%	19%	264
Japan	180%	18%	1,409

NA = not available.

Figure 3. The Problem of Short-Term External Debt

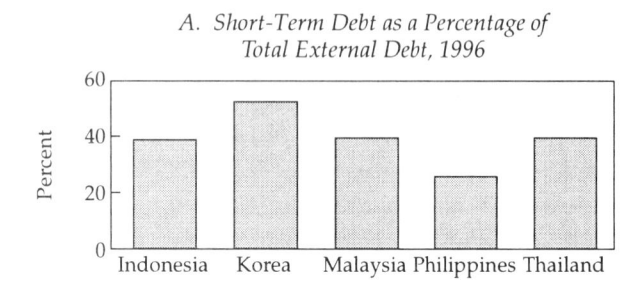

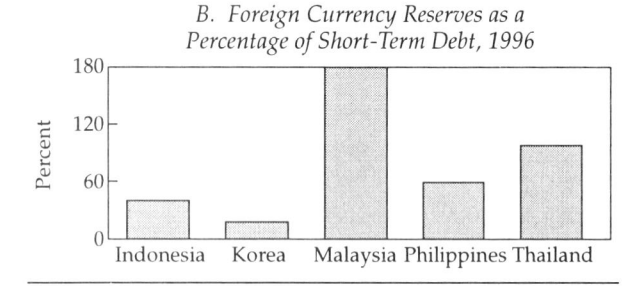

A. Short-Term Debt as a Percentage of Total External Debt, 1996

B. Foreign Currency Reserves as a Percentage of Short-Term Debt, 1996

Asian current-account deficits, especially for Thailand, the Philippines, and Indonesia, were relatively large in 1996, mostly because investment levels were extremely high.

How the current-account deficits were financed is the important factor, because the financing determines, to some extent, a country's vulnerability in a crisis: If the debt inflow is higher than the current-account deficit, the country's debt ratios will increase over time. Figure 4 suggests that the debt ratios for Thailand, Indonesia, and the Philippines were increasing together with their financial vulnerability. Because of the generally optimistic view on the creditworthiness of these countries, the rapid growth these markets were experiencing, and to some extent, the fixed exchange rate regimes of these countries, rising debt inflows largely financed the current-account deficits. The inflows were not simply foreign investors putting debt into the local markets; more importantly, they were the corporations and even banks in these countries borrowing abroad and leaving those currency-exposed liabilities unhedged. This strategy was an attempt to avoid high interest rates in their home markets and attract longer-term foreign currency financing, which on a current-cost basis was cheaper for these borrowers. The strategy was predicated on the belief that the currency regimes would remain fairly stable or would be volatile only within a narrow band, which proved to be unrealistic.

In the future, the profile depicted in Figure 4 will change dramatically. Given the changes in exchange rates in the region, emerging Asia is now probably one of the most attractive places in the world in terms of export competitiveness, which will help shift the current-account deficits sharply into surplus. Already visible is a large shift to current-account surpluses based on the collapse of high-cost imports. Export growth should follow, as long as banks can provide the working capital.

Capital-account flows are also expected to shift away from debt in favor of foreign direct investment. FDI has been relatively high in several of the countries (Malaysia, for example) but relatively low in others (notably, Korea). FDI is basically equity investment and serves to protect bondholders in a crisis. Thus, bond investors will increasingly associate sovereign creditworthiness with such investment, and excessive reliance on debt inflows will moderate over time.

Figure 4. Current-Account Deficits and Debt Inflows as Percentage of GDP, 1996

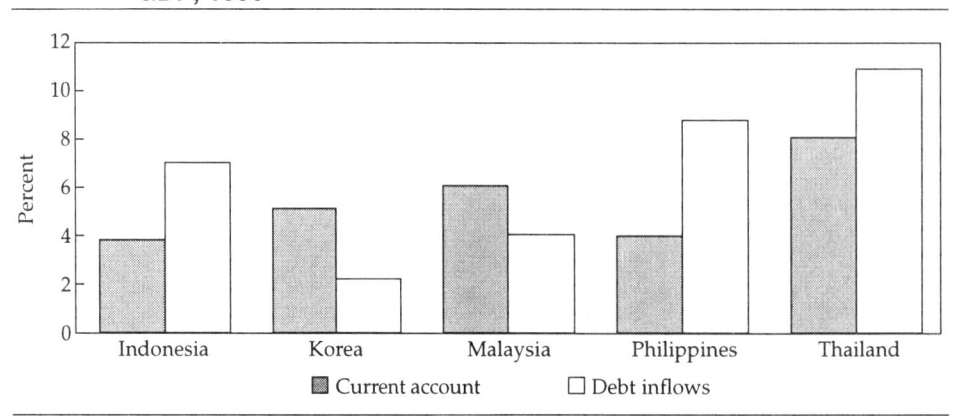

Real Exchange Rates. The final factor contributing to the Asian turmoil is historical movements in real exchange rates. **Figure 5** shows the trend since 1980 in an index based on a regional rate that is the aggregate of the real effective exchange rates of nine emerging Asian economies (weighted by GDPs). In the mid-1980s, on a real effective basis, these countries' exchange rates depreciated dramatically, which, given that most of these countries were not indebted at that time, was largely a contagion response to the Latin crisis occurring at that time. Subsequent to that sharp drop was an upward revaluation; a similar uptick might be expected at the end of the latest sharp devaluation, if and when improvements in real economic performance and central bank policy restore confidence on a sustained basis.

The exchange rate movements indicated in Figure 5 reflect the flows demanded by domestic borrowers in these countries, which are desperate to hedge foreign currency liabilities. The liquidity in most of the currency markets in emerging Asia has been and remains very low, and relatively small flows can greatly affect the quoted exchange rate figures. For instance, in Indonesia, trading of only US$200 million a day in the dollar equivalent of rupiah in the foreign exchange market can affect the rupiah/dollar exchange rate by 2,000–3,000 rupiahs. The implication is that not only is the exchange rate very volatile but the central bank's ability to intervene in the foreign exchange market could be much stronger than the reserve position indicates.

Table 2 shows the huge adjustment in stock valuations that has taken place in the same nine countries since the crisis began; stock prices fell

Table 2. Change in Stock Market Valuation from Previous Year, 1997
(U.S. dollar terms)

Country	Valuation Change
China	–14.2%
Hong Kong	–24.5
Indonesia	–24.5
Korea	–75.0
Malaysia	–64.5
Philippines	–54.5
Singapore	–33.6
Taiwan	–4.2
Thailand	–66.3

substantially and across the board in calendar year 1997. A similar adjustment has occurred in real asset markets—the real estate markets, for example—but the evidence may not yet be visible because some of these markets have no liquidity. For instance, in the Bangkok real estate market, no transactions are occurring. Clearly, if a transaction did occur, it would be at a price far below where the precrisis transaction occurred. Although some markets, notably the Korean stock market, recovered somewhat early in 1998, a sustained recovery will have to await stabilized or even revalued exchange rates, real economic performance, and evidence of structural reforms in these countries.

Lessons

Investors can learn a half dozen lessons from identifying the various factors that contributed to the Asian crisis. The first lesson is the need to focus on external liquidity as well as the debt burden in looking at

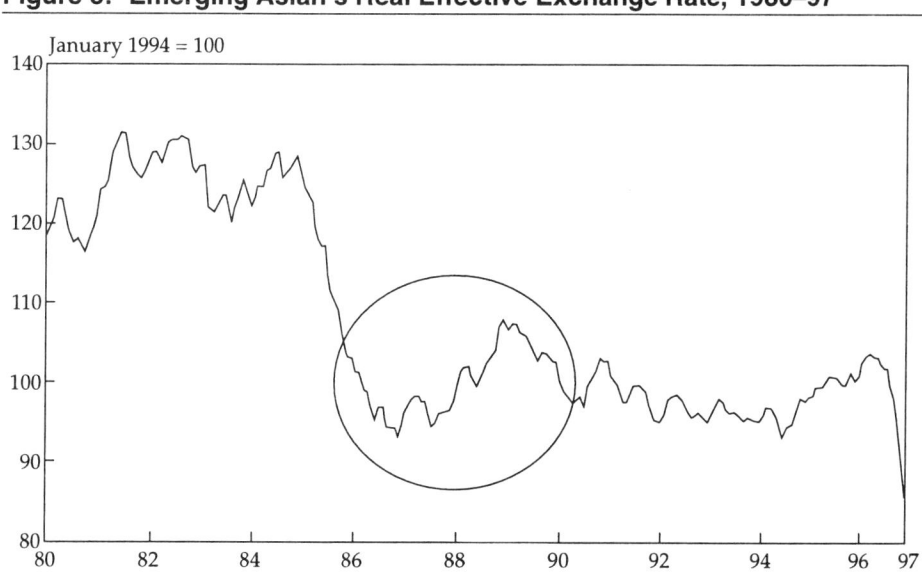

Figure 5. Emerging Asian's Real Effective Exchange Rate, 1980–97

sovereign creditworthiness. In an environment of open capital flows, the most frequently used measures of the debt burdens of sovereigns—that is, external debt as a percentage of GDP or of exports, the total stock of debt, the interest cost of the debt as a percentage of GDP, and debt-service ratios—are all lagging indicators. Such indicators cannot keep up with the sort of fast-moving capital flows that can result from the immediate reaction of investors in times of crisis. The traditional measures are important as a baseline for establishing the relative vulnerability of sovereigns to financial shocks, but measures such as the reserve coverage of short-term debt, the stock of short-term external debt, and the percentage of foreign investors in the local short-term markets will be more useful as leading, or at least concurrent, indicators of potential sovereign problems.

Second, the credibility of government policies is a key factor affecting investor confidence. Analysts can look at a number of objective (largely ratio-driven) factors in assessing sovereign risk, just as they examine financial statement data in corporate analyses. But just as the conclusions of an objective corporate analysis can be turned upside down by management decisions and actions, sovereign analysis also has a subjective component. For instance, based on past experiences, Thailand and Indonesia possessed relatively strong policy credibility going into the crisis. Both had central bank managements that were well regarded internationally, and even in the early stages of the crisis, Indonesia's central bank reacted well—not attempting to defend the exchange rates unwisely by spending all of its reserves and not using monetary policy to tighten interest rates. In the end, however, all that credibility did not help Indonesia. The reality is that the political risks outweighed the financial risks.

Thailand is an example of the best case and the worst case in regard to credibility. Because of relatively high short-term debt, Thailand was the country in Asia that most came under pressure in the currency markets during the 1995 Mexican crisis, and the Thais defended their situation astutely. They devised an appropriate policy mixture of defending the exchange rate and creating a large reservoir of policy credibility. So, when the recent turmoil struck the Asian markets, many observers believed Thailand would efficiently manage its way out of the crisis. In fact, however, in the spring of 1997, Thai government officials embarked on the worst of all possible policy alternatives: defending the currency aggressively, spending almost all the country's reserves without publicizing that action, and then devaluing the currency after swearing repeatedly that they would not do so. The end was a total lack of credibility, to such an extent that the Thais even wasted the positive market perceptions that should have been generated by the International Monetary Fund (IMF) bailout package.

Third, investors should have learned that banking system risk and private internal leverage, even though it is not external debt, directly affect sovereign creditworthiness. The basic reason is that the health of a country's banking system affects the allocation of investments and capital within that country. To the extent that the institutions for allocating funds for investment purposes are poorly designed, as was the case in many of the Asian banking systems, funds will be misallocated and investment capital will be wasted. This issue involves sovereign risk because, in the end, the government is practically, even if not legally, responsible for the soundness of the banking system. A healthy banking system is necessary to facilitate confidence in the economy and to finance corporate working capital at a level sufficient to keep or lift the economy out of recession.

Fourth, the fundamental strength and legitimacy of a political system is fully tested only in a time of crisis. Conventional wisdom has often held that Western-style democracy is not necessary in Asia. Certainly the evidence is that some relatively authoritarian regimes operating in Asia at early stages of development have been conducive to more rapid reforms of institutions than would have been the case in purely democratic societies at early stages of development. But whether an authoritarian regime can command legitimacy in times of crisis is questionable, as can be seen in the current crisis in the contrast between Korea and Thailand, on the one hand, and Indonesia, on the other.

Korea was essentially a military dictatorship in the 1950s and 1960s, the period of its most rapid growth. It has now evolved into a more democratic society, which is to be expected given the increase in per capita income in the country. This continuing evolution is cause for optimism that Korea will work its way through the current crisis. There has been a change in government, and the signals at this point are supportive of rigorous reforms. More importantly, the election process gives the government that is putting the reforms in place legitimacy in the eyes of the Korean people. Without that legitimacy, enacting sweeping reforms in the inevitably tough times that lie ahead for Korea would be difficult.

Indonesia is a total contrast to Korea with respect to political legitimacy. The Suharto government has provided stability for a number of years and has clearly presided over enormous economic development. The legitimacy of the Suharto government rests heavily on its track record of developing real improvements in income, however, an improvement that is not occurring now and will not occur in the foreseeable future. In fact, real deterioration has occurred in living standards that has not yet been fully felt. Moreover, the system in Indonesia does not provide for a smooth change in leadership, and the resulting uncertainty is definitely affecting the orderly outcome of the Indonesian debt crisis.

The fifth lesson is drawn uniquely from Korea: Bond investors have essentially been protected by bank creditors, and the latter actually face the greater risk of default. Bond investors are now a major part of the flows of debt to emerging markets, unlike in the 1980s when all lending activity was basically syndicated loans by bankers. But commercial banks clearly have provided some support for bond investors during the current crisis, not from price changes but in terms of actual default risk. For example, a rating agency would classify the recent Korean bank restructuring agreement as an in-practice default on bank obligations, even though final terms have not yet been defined. J.P. Morgan, one of many parties to the agreement, will probably exchange its current debt for some new one-, two-, or three-year loans guaranteed by the Korean government; because J.P. Morgan really had no choice in the matter, that deal is essentially a default, a default experienced by the banks but not by the bondholders. The bottom line for a government issuer is to decide which parties will be easiest to negotiate with. Bondholders usually account for a smaller part of the total debt, are hard to find, and are protected by legal documents that are relatively complicated for the issuer to restructure, all of which makes putting pressure on bondholders difficult for the issuer in a workout scenario. In contrast, the government knows the commercial bank well in most cases and knows also that the bank probably wants to have an ongoing presence in that country. So, governments are much more likely to try to pressure bank creditors than bondholders to renegotiate loan terms. In the case of Korea, the preferability of dealing with the banks was particularly obvious because of the clear need for some short-term debt to be transferred into long-term debt, which is easier to accomplish from a legal and practical point of view when dealing with commercial bank counterparties than with bond investors.

An unanswered question is whether the pressure for accommodation brought by governments will cause banks to rein in their lending activities in these markets or whether those banks will continue their support at historical levels. If one result of the crisis is that banks become less willing to lend to these countries in the syndicated markets and more reluctant to take the exposures in the sizes and at the spreads they did previously, then support and protection for bond investors will diminish. And without bank support, restructuring and workouts become an entirely new ball game; that is, no one has ever had to really restructure a sovereign bond, because relatively few such bonds existed in Latin America and those bonds remained current even during the 1980s debt crisis.

Regional Outlook

Despite the current dislocations, the longer-term fundamentals in Asia remain positive. The factors that led to above-average growth and stellar economic performance for the past 30 years—high domestic savings rates and fiscal conservatism—remain in place. The near-term outlook for Asian credit, however, depends on the establishment or continuation of several key trends.

The expected restructuring of the banking sectors will lead to more local bond activity in these countries. Now, the allocation of credit is heavily mediated through the banking system in the form of straight loans, with most investors or households in these countries having to rely on bank deposits as their choice for an investment. In the future, however, both the sovereign and corporate bond markets in these countries must, and probably will, broaden and deepen as governments move into deficit financing and banking systems are restructured.

Transparency and openness in disclosure of financial information must greatly improve. Latin American governments and corporate issuers learned from Latin America's crisis in 1995 the importance of talking to and cultivating investors. Asian issuers are in the process of learning that same lesson—the hard way—and disclosure will improve as a result.

Credit spreads have already recovered to some extent, but continued improvement depends on the speed of reforms and how sustained the reform momentum turns out to be. How quickly will the Asian countries embark on meaningful reforms? There has been a lot of tough talk from the various governments, but evidence of implementation must be forthcoming. The Western approach would be to cure such serious problems with a short, sharp adjustment that would provide the underpinnings for a future period of growth. Unfortunately, the tendency in some of these countries is to act only very deliberately over a long period of time and only after trying to achieve a consensus or compromise on difficult decisions. This approach risks a prolonged slowdown and a long period of wide credit spreads.

The Pacific area provides a prime example of this difference in philosophy. In the early 1990s, banking crises occurred almost simultaneously in Australia and Japan. The Japanese banking crisis continues unabated, with the only real question being whether US$800 billion or US$1.2 trillion dollars will be needed to bail out the Japanese banking system. Australia's banks, however, are quite healthy now because the Australian banking system, which had problem loans of similar magnitude (as a percentage of GDP), particularly in the property sector, "bit the bullet" early in many respects and was out of its crisis within two years.

Taking into account these factors, J.P. Morgan's view is that 1998 will be the trough year in terms of GDP growth in emerging Asia. **Table 3** suggests 2.9 percent real GDP growth for the six countries listed, compared with the more than 6 percent experienced in 1997 and slightly more than 5 percent expected in 1999. However, there are big differences between countries. China is clearly going to be the growth driver, even though that 7.5 percent real GDP growth looks like a recession by recent Chinese standards. The three recipients of IMF bailout assistance—Indonesia, Thailand, and Korea—will have fairly serious recessions in the context of their historical performance; the –2 percent growth rate is more or less a depression in Korea, which for many years was accustomed to 5–7 percent average growth. The depth of the downturn is going to be substantial, but what is important is that every one of these countries except Malaysia is expected to experience some rebound in growth in 1999. Malaysia, although it has had some of the same currency and internal debt problems as other countries, has not yet faced the same degree of external pressure, the same type of balance-of-payments crisis; unfortunately, its recessionary time will be delayed until 1999.

Table 3. Forecasts for Growth in Real GDP

Country	1997	1998	1999
China	9.0%	7.5%	7.4%
Korea	6.1	–2.0	3.5
Indonesia	7.0	–4.0	3.5
Malaysia	7.5	3.0	–1.0
Philippines	5.0	1.6	4.1
Thailand	0.5	–3.5	3.5
Regional average	6.4%	2.9%	5.1%

Specific Country Views

The overall view is that long-term prospects for Asia are still positive and that 1999 will be the year when recovery begins for most of the region. But substantial differences exist among the individual countries.

China. China has external strength but internal weakness. Many investors wonder whether China will be the next domino to fall in Asia; the parallels with other countries in the region are obvious—a poor banking system, an authoritarian government, opaque disclosure, and an essentially fixed currency regime. The currency is not likely to be depreciated at the moment, however, because of China's singular characteristics. The currency is not traded and thus not vulnerable to speculative pressure, and the current account is in a surplus position. As shown in **Table 4**, external debt, which is mostly medium and long term in nature, is relatively small, less than 70 percent of exports and less than 20 percent of GDP. The stock of cash reserves is more than three times the short-term debt. In fact, the cash reserves also exceed the total debt, so China could pay all its debt back immediately if anybody asked. Given these circumstances, a balance-of-payments crisis in China is unlikely and immediate pressure on the Chinese currency (and economy in general) is small.

Table 4. China: Key Forecast Data

Factor	1997	1998	1999
GDP growth (%)	9.0	7.5	7.4
Inflation (consumer price index, %)	2.9	1.9	3.2
Fiscal balance to GDP (%)	–1.0	–1.2	–1.5
Current account to GDP (%)	2.8	1.3	0.0
External debt to GDP (%)	17.1	15.9	14.9
External debt to exports (%)	69.7	68.2	65.3
Reserves to short-term external debt (%)	339.0	311.0	265.0
Debt-service ratio (×)	8.6	9.3	9.0
New debt to GDP (%)	1.4	1.1	1.2

Even so, now that Southeast Asia has devalued so substantially, some investors fear that China, facing the prospect of becoming noncompetitive vis-à-vis exports from Thailand, Indonesia, or Korea, will follow suit. One reason such devaluation is unlikely is that the current account is now in surplus, and it is likely to become balanced rather than go into deficit, so the government will have little inclination or financial need to devalue. Two other reasons that make devaluation unlikely are even more compelling. First, the relationship with the United States is important to the Chinese leadership. The last thing China wants to do is aggravate the already unfavorable trade picture they have with the United States. Second, devaluing the currency would stoke inflation in China, and major incidents of opposition to the central government, such as Tianamen Square, have always occurred in periods of high inflation in China. The Chinese government is committed to avoiding increasing inflation whatever the cost. Controlling inflation and keeping growth at a relatively high level are the government's top priorities.

The lesson that Chinese leaders should be learning from the current crisis in Asia is that they should accelerate reform of their financial system, which needs to be well developed and competitive before the country opens its capital account to external capital flows. Also, the government has been gradually reforming the state-owned enterprise sector, which consists of many inefficient state-owned companies, but the reforms need to be accelerated.

The political system seems to be stable, but its legitimacy is based on delivering real economic growth to the average Chinese person. If investors are comfortable with the current economic stewardship of China, they should be relatively comfortable with the current political leadership; the political system becomes a risk only if a major economic downturn occurs. Eventually, if China becomes richer, a strong demand to liberalize and become more democratic will develop, but such change will not occur for 5–10 years.

Hong Kong. Hong Kong has a somewhat higher sovereign credit rating than China. Hong Kong's ability to pay its foreign debt is even better than China's; although politically the government is now orchestrated by China to some extent, the external ability to service debt is linked to Hong Kong's own level of reserves and independent management of those reserves. The currency peg to the U.S. dollar will be maintained; the peg is an absolute currency board system, which is highly desirable from a currency management perspective if the government and the central bank are willing to allow natural adjustments, particularly rising interest rates and falling asset prices, to occur within the economy. The Hong Kong currency board has exhibited that willingness.

In fact, Hong Kong's policy credibility in general is high by Asian standards. In the recent crisis atmosphere, in contrast to the rest of Asia, where policymakers have been either inept at explaining themselves or unavailable for explanations, the Hong Kong monetary authorities willingly, eagerly, and effectively explained to anyone who wanted to listen why they were doing what they were doing, and their explanations made a compelling argument for what is good for Hong Kong in the long term. Because of Hong Kong's willingness to pursue appropriate policies, the major asset-price risks currently lie in the property sector and, to some extent, in the banking sector. But in contrast to the rest of Asia, Hong Kong is essentially a developed country with sophisticated banking systems and relatively well-capitalized property companies.

Potential Chinese interference in the Hong Kong economy is probably overstated, but Hong Kong could lose some of its function as a transition port between Taiwan and China. As China opens more to the rest of the world, and particularly when direct links between Taiwan and China are developed, more of Taiwan's considerable trade with China that now goes through Hong Kong could go directly to cost-competitive ports in the Pearl River estuary.

Indonesia. In many respects, Indonesia is no weaker than other Asian countries. For instance, its currency and banking system problems, although severe, are not much more severe than the problems being experienced elsewhere in the region. **Table 5** gives some clues to the mixed nature of Indonesia's prospects. The external debt level is expected to decline, but it is among the highest in the region. On the other hand, the structure of the external debt is favorable, in that the government's own debt burden is not particularly onerous because most of the debt is owed to bilateral and multilateral lenders at advantageous interest rates. Reserve coverage of short-term debt is actually quite high, and the trend of the current account is expected to be toward increasing surplus. Inflation, although expected to decline by 1999, will nevertheless remain high, and recovery in GDP growth will be among the slowest in the region.

Table 5. Indonesia: Key Forecast Data

Factor	1997	1998	1999
GDP growth (%)	7.0	–4.0	3.5
Inflation (consumer price index, %)	6.8	18.0	12.0
Fiscal balance to GDP (%)	–1.0	–1.5	0.0
Current account to GDP (%)	–4.5	3.9	5.2
External debt to GDP (%)	64.2	130.7	97.3
External debt to exports (%)	197.5	182.4	160.6
Reserves to short-term external debt (%)	83.0	140.0	182.0
Debt-service ratio (×)	31.9	30.4	25.2
New debt to GDP (%)	12.7	21.8	6.7

What makes Indonesia so difficult to analyze is not so much the economic data as the political environment. An immediate concern is the opaque nature of the political system and the policy-making apparatus. The fact that the institutions of government within Indonesia are not forthcoming with information and explanations does not promote confidence in any transition process. For instance, tracking changes in reserve management or monetary policy is difficult to impossible, so conclusions about the government's currency management are suspect at best.

The more important issue is the Suharto regime's legitimacy in the eyes of Indonesians. The Suharto government is not loved by Indonesians, but it is respected. After taking power in the mid-1960s, the Suharto government took a large, ethnically diverse, extremely poor country and steadily developed it. Memories of the last transition of power in 1965 are fresh in the minds of most Indonesians, who clearly desire to avoid a repeat of that type of ethnic conflict. Thus, in the current environment, the decisions of the Suharto regime are basically designed to maintain social stability within the economy, which could jeopardize the pace of reforms necessary to get the economy back on a healthy footing. For example, the IMF and Indonesia have agreed that elimination of a variety of price subsidies is necessary, but as a practical matter, in an economy that will experience a threefold increase in unemployment in the next several months, eliminating the subsidy on kerosene, a key commodity for the rural population in Indonesia, is not politically feasible.

Not only will such social/political constraints slow reforms, but Indonesia has great hidden potential for social conflict. For example, the full impact of the economic slowdown has not fully translated into company behavior with respect to employees. So, job losses will mount; price increases are already flowing through in terms of inflationary impact, but many more increases will follow. All these developments will adversely affect the large, relatively poor rural population and increase the risk for social unrest, which could lead to violence.

In addition, several major problems exist in the private sector. First, private-sector Indonesian companies have borrowed abroad on a short-term basis, and much of this borrowing was in the form of promissory notes that were never registered with the central bank. This borrowing activity, which came to light only recently, is estimated to total US$15 billion to US$20 billion. The currency depreciation already experienced, plus any further devaluations, puts enormous pressures on these borrowers—thus, the potential for massive defaults. The fact that so much of the short-term external indebtedness in Indonesia is held by private corporations and the sheer size of that debt also make a banking agreement like the one worked out in Korea unlikely in Indonesia. Another private-sector constraint is the widespread lack of working capital, which reduces both corporate and governmental ability to boost trade and build current surpluses. Also of concern is the lack of disclosure and reliable financial information. Indonesian companies are no more forthcoming than the Indonesian government.

A final (perhaps ominous) note of concern is that, whereas all countries in the region face problems, Indonesia is the only country that is experiencing capital flight. It is different from the capital flight that happened in Latin America 20 years ago; then, the flight occurred when wealthy people moved their money out of the country in advance of impending hyperinflation. The wealthy people of Indonesia are either Chinese or connected in some way to the Suharto regime, and both groups apparently see the economic turmoil as a harbinger of social turmoil and are moving capital out of the country. Economic difficulties in Indonesia have historically resulted in ethnic attacks against Chinese residents, which have already been reported, and such difficulties may also bring violence against the government. If substantial and sustained, the current capital flight will put additional pressure on the Indonesian rupiah.

Korea. South Korea is on the road to recovery but is not there yet. The recently negotiated bank agreement was comprehensive in fixing the short-term debt problem, but other issues have constrained the rate of improvement in spreads to date. (Ironically, in Korea's case, some improvements in perceived creditworthiness could have occurred by just changing the maturity structure of the debt rather than coming up with a solution for reducing it; this effect was not possible in other countries in the region, especially Indonesia.)

The expectations are that Korea's current-account and trade balance, which were in deficit by as much as US$20 billion to US$25 billion a year in past years, will move strongly into surplus in 1998. As indicated in our forecasts in **Table 6**, J.P. Morgan expects the current-account balance to go from −2 percent of GDP in 1997 to 6+ percent of GDP in 1998, which is equivalent to inflows of capital of about US$20 billion on an annual basis—a very positive inflow.

Table 6. Korea: Key Forecast Data

Factor	1997	1998	1999
GDP growth (%)	6.1	−2.0	3.5
Inflation (consumer price index, %)	4.4	12.0	6.0
Fiscal balance to GDP (%)	−2.3	−3.0	−3.2
Current account to GDP (%)	−2.0	6.6	6.6
External debt to GDP (%)	34.0	55.1	43.6
External debt to exports (%)	87.1	87.4	80.0
Reserves to short-term external debt (%)	28.0	72.0	112.0
Debt-service ratio (×)	10.9	14.1	15.7
New debt to GDP (%)	7.3	13.0	5.6

The fiscal position in Korea is expected to deteriorate because of the need for bank assistance. Of all the Asian countries except Japan, Korea is going to have the largest need for a bank bailout by the government. It will probably be well in excess of US$100 billion over the next several years and will have to be financed mostly by debt, probably in the domestic market. This debt need not increase external indebtedness by the government, but it does imply a cost to the government of financing the debt of 3–4 percent of GDP annually. So, in order to keep its fiscal position strong, Korea will have to either cut spending or raise taxes to offset the large deterioration in the debt position. The need for substantial policy changes is probably factored into current Korean credit ratings, which have plummeted for a variety of reasons, including the fact that the bank restructuring will have a direct impact on fiscal creditworthiness. The positive side is that Korea has some flexibility in debt capacity because of low government debt levels.

The new Korean government is committed to reform, perhaps even radically so, which is a good sign. Still, the key to how fast and how far Korea recovers will be the speed of corporate restructuring, particularly of the large *chaebol* conglomerates. The banking system is an obvious concern, but controlling the banks is much easier for the government than controlling how the *chaebol* restructure themselves or convincing the *chaebol* managers to sell off large parts of their organizations to reduce debt. Some news with respect to labor reform has been encouraging, but whether the populace at large has bought into the need for widespread labor-market reform is not clear.

From a ratings point of view, Korea is already being upgraded back to the top of the BB category by several of the rating agencies, and an upgrade back into the investment-grade category is possible. Such a rise in rating will depend heavily on the pace and substantive nature of corporate restructuring, however, and the delivery on reform promises by the government. An upgrade to investment grade is not likely before 1999.

Malaysia. Malaysia has avoided a balance-of-payments crisis largely because of its external strength. **Table 7** shows that Malaysia's external debt is relatively low and is expected to decline. The reserve coverage of short-term debt is high and is expected to increase. By most external liquidity measures, Malaysia looks markedly less vulnerable than the three countries that have needed IMF assistance (Korea, Indonesia, and Thailand). Table 7 reveals a large current-account deficit, but it is expected to move to surplus as a result of FDI inflows.

The primary risk in Malaysia lies in the banking system. The Malaysian banking system has the same degree of credit overextension as the Korean and Thai banking systems. The Malaysian banking system, however, has relatively good margins and a relatively strong capital base, which enhances the system's ability to withstand the large write-offs that are inevitable. Nonetheless, the potential exists that the government will have to provide support to some institutions, particularly the small banks and some finance companies. Most of the lending in Malaysia has been in an overheated property market and on a highly leveraged basis. Much lending was also based on shares as collateral, and with the stock market down about 50 percent from precrisis levels, the value of that collateral is obviously in doubt. The overleveraging in both sectors will undoubtedly haunt corporations and banks in Malaysia through at least 1999.

As of February 1998, the government has kept monetary policy relatively easy, which has mitigated the effect on borrowers of the high interest rates that would have been expected in this environment but which also risks a more painful correction in late 1998 or in 1999. Whereas most other countries in the region will have worked through their problems by that time, Malaysia may well be still in the midst of, or even only beginning, its period of economic turmoil.

The political system is also somewhat of a wild card in forecasting Malaysian behavior and performance. The political regime is relatively stable, but nationalistic stances and policies are still possible, as evidenced by last year's accusations by the Malaysian prime minister that foreign speculators were ruining his country. Investors should be concerned about such nationalistic tendencies getting in the way of good economic practices; for example, might the leading Malaysian oil company, Petronas, be asked to bail out more troubled companies in Malaysia because it is financially strong?

Thailand. Thailand is probably a midlevel credit in the region; its problems have now been overshadowed, first, by Korea and, later, by Indonesia. But no simple, aggressive solution to Thailand's long-term problems has yet been found. One plus for Thailand, especially compared with Indonesia, is the political system: The new Thai government has substantial political legitimacy. Although the speed of reforms is unclear, the legitimacy derived from having gone to the voters gives the new government some ability to implement policy changes and reforms.

Two keys to solving the pervasive bad-loan problems in Thailand are restructuring the banks and clarifying the bankruptcy process. Bank restructuring is actually progressing well; the smaller banks have

Table 7. Malaysia: Key Forecast Data

Factor	1997	1998	1999
GDP growth (%)	7.5	3.0	−1.0
Inflation (consumer price index, %)	2.7	6.5	5.0
Fiscal balance to GDP (%)	0.0	−1.5	−2.0
Current account to GDP (%)	−9.4	−6.0	6.9
External debt to GDP (%)	41.3	52.5	47.5
External debt to exports (%)	38.2	35.4	31.7
Reserves to short-term external debt (%)	168.0	165.0	196.0
Debt-service ratio (×)	5.9	5.8	53.7
New debt to GDP (%)	5.3	5.6	2.5

been restructured, and the government has taken over many problem banks and is in the process of cleaning them up. An ongoing problem in Thailand is the fact that, although the country has bankruptcy laws, the legal system is extremely slow and a bank holding collateral interest in a defaulted property developer has difficulty getting any kind of satisfaction. It may take five to seven years to get possession of a property, which creates an incentive for banks to make deals with troubled borrowers. Such a system implies that price adjustments in the property sector in Thailand will be slow to materialize.

Thailand's liquidity is improving, but as shown in **Table 8**, its external debt is quite high. The current account is expected to be in surplus in both 1998 and 1999, but external debt is well over 100 percent of exports. (In the case of Thailand, and probably the rest of Asia, external debt as a percentage of exports is more meaningful than the traditionally used external debt as a percentage of GDP; the latter, which is normally calculated in U.S. dollar terms, is very volatile because of exchange rate fluctuations.) Thailand's debt burden suggests an environment in which capital is relatively costly, which will make financing its large infrastructure needs a great challenge.

Conclusion

Asia is truly going through a period of pronounced crisis. Asian leaders can and should take to heart lessons learned by policymakers in past crises in other regions—the need for openness and transparency, the need to modernize the financial system, and the need to cultivate investors. If they do, a rehabilitation of Asia will occur, and many (maybe all) of the countries in the region will once again provide a fundamentally strong economic environment for both sovereign and corporate credits.

Bond investors who take the time to study and understand the nature and causes of the Asian crisis and who learn the unique lessons imparted by that crisis will be in a position to take full advantage of those attractive postcrisis opportunities.

Table 8. Thailand: Key Forecast Data

Factor	1997	1998	1999
GDP growth (%)	0.5	−3.5	3.5
Inflation (consumer price index, %)	5.6	12.0	8.0
Fiscal balance to GDP (%)	−1.0	−2.0	−1.0
Current account to GDP (%)	−4.2	8.4	7.7
External debt to GDP (%)	66.6	94.3	79.4
External debt to exports (%)	126.3	124.0	117.3
Reserves to short-term external debt (%)	90.0	114.0	129.0
Debt-service ratio (×)	14.7	12.9	13.3
New debt to GDP (%)	11.6	15.7	7.1

Question and Answer Session

John Paulsen

Question: How do you reconcile currency devaluation and continuing money supply growth with your relatively low inflation forecasts for most of these Asian countries?

Paulsen: There is considerable debate within J.P. Morgan about how much inflation is going to rise in the region. Some differences of opinion come down to whether we use inflation figures that are created by the countries themselves, based on various baskets of goods in various countries, or whether we try to generate our own estimates. For those inflation baskets, the ingredients and prices that go into them from many of the countries—Malaysia, for example—are manipulated, so the inflation figures are artificial to some extent.

The basic question is whether we expect to see *hyperinflation* in Asia. Indonesia probably has a high risk for hyperinflation, but otherwise, that inflationary scenario seems unlikely in the region. For one thing, the region has no history of hyperinflation, and for another, the shrinkage in imports reduces the risk of importing high inflation. Our inflation forecasts may be on the low side and may well be adjusted upwards, but the likelihood of widespread hyperinflation is minimal.

Question: Why did the lessons learned in the Mexican crisis not help avert the Asian crisis?

Paulsen: Although similarities can be found, the two crises have fundamentally different causes. The Mexican crisis evolved from the speculative excesses of "hot" money being attracted to a local currency, with hedge funds and other risk factors thrown into the mix. The Asian crisis, in contrast, is at its heart the result of the volatility of commercial bank exposures to rollovers of external, especially short-term, debt. These countries and many others (in Western Europe, for example) had experienced high short-term debt levels for many years without untoward consequences for investors, so investors were not looking at that debt and the resulting exposures as a source of problems. What they were looking for, the speculative excesses remembered from the Mexican crisis, did not exist in the same way.

Question: What are the ramifications of a possible debt moratorium in the Asian region for the Japanese banking system, and what is your outlook for Japanese sovereign risk?

Paulsen: Japanese banks have high exposures to Indonesian corporations. Their Korean loans have largely been restructured, and the quality is fairly high within the context of the region. All of the Asian loss exposures faced by Japanese banks combined are minuscule compared with their own domestic exposures, which are principally the result of bad property lending and which run into the hundreds of billions of dollars.

I believe Japan does not face a risk of downgrade. Certainly, the situation contains some negative factors—the weak banking system, the lack of disclosure, the slow pace of institutional reform, a weakening fiscal condition—but Japan is one of the three largest economies in the world and one of the three most creditworthy in the world. The external strength of the Japanese economy, with reserves in excess of US$200 billion, is quite strong, and the yen is one of the three hard currencies used globally. The bottom line is that Japan is a major international creditor country, and as long as it remains so, there are relatively few arguments for a downgrade in Japan's credit rating.

Question: How can these countries obtain the financing they need to export their way out of a banking crisis?

Paulsen: Countries cannot simply export their way out of their problems. Structural changes are also needed. But export activity does play a role, especially in the near term. In most of the region, enough improvement in perceptions of creditworthiness has occurred to enable some improvement in liquidity and access to needed working capital.

The problem exists primarily in Indonesia. Indonesia's perceived creditworthiness is so low that it has had difficulty convincing foreign financial institutions even to provide letters of credit to finance imports of necessary food stuffs. Similarly, the domestic banking system is not providing the liquidity necessary for exporters to build up working capital to increase exports.

These countries do not need additional fixed-asset investment for manufacturing capacity; the ability to provide goods for export is already there to a large extent. What they need is working capital; with the notable exception of Indonesia, most countries in the region should be on the rebound in this regard.

Question: Which of these countries is most at risk should the economies of the developed countries experience a slowdown?

Paulsen: We would likely see a broad-based weakness in Asia in that scenario. I doubt that any one particular country is weaker than the others except perhaps Malaysia or South Korea. They might suffer somewhat more because their products tend to be the high-value-added type that competes directly with West European and U.S. products. The primary threat to this region from the developed economies is not simply a growth slowdown but that the developed countries will put in place more trade barriers to fight what they see to be predatory import competition against their domestic industries.

Self-Evaluation Examination

1. Ashur includes which of the following as major elements of sovereign credit analysis?
   I. Issuer liquidity.
   II. Increased privatization.
   III. External accounts management.
   IV. Development of local markets.
   A. I and III only.
   B. II and IV only.
   C. II, III, and IV only.
   D. I, II, III, and IV.

2. According to Ashur, qualitative risk assessment includes:
   A. Domestic fiscal management.
   B. A country's financial needs for non-domestic currency.
   C. The breakdown of a country's long- and short-term debt.
   D. Central bank independence.

3. Credit policies, bankruptcy laws, supervisory stance, and accounting quality are all aspects of which of the following areas of sovereign analysis?
   A. Political framework.
   B. Currency management.
   C. Banking-sector solvency.
   D. Sovereign recognition of problems.

4. Which of the following actions will not occur until 2002 if monetary union in Europe continues as planned?
   A. Securities will be redenominated or renominalized.
   B. National currencies will be retired.
   C. Settlement and pricing will be conducted in euros.
   D. National exchange rates will be permanently fixed to the euro.

5. Flannery contends that implementation of the European Monetary Union (EMU) will make the member capital markets more efficient by:
   I. Enabling capital to move more freely.
   II. Eliminating within-market currency risk.
   III. Providing greater depth and liquidity.
   IV. Fostering disintermediation.
   A. I only.
   B. III only.
   C. II and IV only.
   D. I, II, III, and IV.

6. According to Flannery, which of the following are continuing risks to successful EMU implementation and performance?
   I. Potential addition of member countries.
   II. Sustainability of the EMU's unified fiscal policy.
   III. Ability of member countries to maintain "fiscal religion."
   IV. Breakdown or delay in unification because of nationalistic feelings.
   A. I only.
   B. I and II only.
   C. II, III, and IV only.
   D. I, II, III, and IV.

7. Which of the following most accurately characterizes the credit-rating momentum for East European sovereigns classified by Vasan as Tier 1 credits?

	Positive Momentum	Negative Momentum
A.	Hungary	Poland
B.	Czech Republic	Hungary
C.	Slovak Republic	Czech Republic
D.	Poland	Slovak Republic

8. Tier 1 East European sovereign credits are characterized by:
   I. Macroeconomic stabilization.
   II. Microeconomic stabilization.
   III. Relatively high levels of foreign direct investment.
   IV. Clear consensus about economic policy.
   A. I and II only.
   B. II and IV only.
   C. I, III, and IV only.
   D. I, II, III, and IV.

9. According to Vasan, an unresolved credit concern that extends across Tier 1 and Tier 2 East European sovereign credits is:
   A. The political role played by military forces.
   B. Weak banking systems.
   C. Bondholder dependence on "good princes."
   D. Large fiscal deficits.

©Association for Investment Management and Research

10. Larson shows that the share of African and Middle Eastern economies in total world trade is:
    A. Less than 10 percent but increasing.
    B. Greater than 10 percent and increasing.
    C. Less than 10 percent and declining.
    D. Greater than 10 percent but declining.

11. Which of the following countries in Africa and the Middle East is the largest issuer of foreign currency bonds?
    A. Israel.
    B. Saudi Arabia.
    C. South Africa.
    D. Turkey.

12. Larson identifies which of the following Arab Gulf countries as having been involved directly or indirectly in foreign currency bond issuance?
    A. Qatar and Oman.
    B. Saudi Arabia and Kuwait.
    C. Kuwait and the United Arab Emirates.
    D. Bahrain and Saudi Arabia.

13. The possibility of a sovereign intervening directly or indirectly in markets in a way that affects companies' ability to meet offshore obligations is an aspect of sovereign risk also known as:
    A. Intermediary risk.
    B. Transfer risk.
    C. Country risk.
    D. Policy risk.

14. Feinland Katz identifies all of the following to be determinants of a Latin American company's competitive position *except*:
    A. Trade barriers.
    B. Regulatory risk.
    C. Capital structure.
    D. Local industry structure.

15. Feinland Katz states that the Latin American country that has a relatively well-developed local capital market *and* relatively strong legal protections of bondholder rights is:
    A. Argentina.
    B. Brazil.
    C. Chile.
    D. Mexico.

16. Paulsen contends that the recent Asian financial crisis can be attributed in part to:
    A. Inefficient investment and low domestic savings rates in the region.
    B. Inefficient investment, but not low domestic savings rates, in the region.
    C. Low domestic savings rates, but not inefficient investment, in the region.
    D. Neither inefficient investment nor low domestic savings rates in the region.

17. Which of the following Asian countries is likely to experience the largest need for debt-financed government assistance to troubled banks?
    A. Indonesia.
    B. Malaysia.
    C. South Korea.
    D. Thailand.

18. Paulsen characterizes which of the following Asian countries as having external strength but internal weakness?
    A. China.
    B. Hong Kong.
    C. Korea.
    D. Thailand.

Self-Evaluation Answers

1. A. Ashur describes four major elements of sovereign credit analysis. They include assessment of the sovereign's liquidity and external accounts management but not assessment of privatization levels or development of local markets.

2. D. Qualitative risk assessment includes ascertaining the independence of a country's central bank. The other three measures are part of quantifiable risk assessment.

3. C. Ashur discusses the need for analysis in all four areas if one is to anticipate changes in sovereign credit. But the four aspects cited in the question relate specifically to assessing the solvency of a country's banking sector.

4. B. Flannery points out that the European Monetary Union will issue new euro coins and currency in the first six months of 2002 and the member currencies will be retired and withdrawn.

5. D. European capital markets are likely to experience all four changes from unification.

6. C. Flannery notes that the potential *withdrawal*, not addition, of a country or countries is a risk to the success of the EMU.

7. D. Vasan characterizes credit-rating momentum as positive for Poland and Hungary but negative for the Czech Republic and the Slovak Republic.

8. C. Vasan cautions that, although privatization programs are in place, microeconomic stabilization has yet to be fully or permanently achieved.

9. B. The economic policies put in place in the region by the so-called Washington consensus do not address the pervasive problem of extremely weak banking systems.

10. C. These regions' share of total world trade declined from 6.7 percent in 1990 to 5.5 percent in 1996.

11. D. Larson states that Turkey has nearly US$15 billion in foreign currency bonds outstanding.

12. A. Although all Gulf Cooperation Council countries are increasingly likely to be potential customers for global capital markets, only Qatar and Oman have so far actually been involved in foreign currency bond issuance.

13. B. Feinland Katz defines this possibility as transfer risk.

14. C. Capital structure is an important determinant of a company's *financial* position, which Feinland Katz distinguishes from the company's competitive position.

15. C. Chile exhibits both characteristics: Its well-developed local capital market is evidence of Chile's positive sovereign policies, and the legal protection of bondholders is evidence of financial flexibility.

16. B. Domestic savings rates in Asia have been relatively high and increasing, but investment activity, although at a high level, has been inefficiently financed.

17. C. Paulsen estimates that recapitalization of Korean banks' nonperforming loans could cost US$155 billion in the next several years.

18. A. Because of its strong external position, China faces little risk of a balance-of-payments crisis, but the slow pace of reform and the continued legitimacy of the political system are matters of concern.

Selected Publications

AIMR

AIMR Performance Presentation Standards Handbook, 2nd edition, 1997

Asian Equity Investing, 1998

Deregulation of the Electric Utility Industry, 1997

Derivatives in Portfolio Management, 1998

Economic Analysis for Investment Professionals, 1997

Equity Research and Valuation Techniques, 1998

Finding Reality in Reported Earnings, 1997

Global Bond Management, 1997

Implementing Global Equity Strategy: Spotlight on Asia, 1997

Investing in Small-Cap and Microcap Securities, 1997

Investing Worldwide VIII: Developments in Global Portfolio Management, 1997

Managing Currency Risk, 1997

Standards of Practice Casebook, 1996

Standards of Practice Handbook, 7th edition, 1996

Research Foundation

Blockholdings of Investment Professionals, 1997
by Sanjai Bhagat, Bernard S. Black, and Margaret M. Blair

Company Performance and Measures of Value Added, 1996
by Pamela P. Peterson, CFA, and David R. Peterson

Controlling Misfit Risk in Multiple-Manager Investment Programs, 1998
by Jeffery V. Bailey, CFA, and David E. Tierney

Country Risk in Global Financial Management, 1997
by Claude B. Erb, CFA, Campbell R. Harvey, and Tadas E. Viskanta

Economic Foundations of Capital Market Returns, 1997
by Brian D. Singer, CFA, and Kevin Terhaar, CFA

Initial Dividends and Implications for Investors, 1997
by James W. Wansley, CFA, William R. Lane, CFA, and Phillip R. Daves

Interest Rate Modeling and the Risk Premiums in Interest Rate Swaps, 1997
Robert Brooks, CFA

Sales-Driven Franchise Value, 1997
Martin L. Leibowitz